Pleiadian Principles for Living

Pleiadian Principles for Living

A Guide to Accessing Dimensional Energies,
Communicating With the Pleiadians,
and Navigating These Changing Times

By Christine Day

New Page Books
A Division of The Career Press, Inc.
Pompton Plains, NJ

PLEIADIAN PRINCIPLES FOR LIVING
EDITED AND TYPESET BY GINA TALUCCI
Cover design by Lucia Rossman
Printed in the U.S.A.

To order this title, please call toll-free 1-800-CAREER-1 (NJ and Canada: 201-848-0310) to order using VISA or MasterCard, or for further information on books from Career Press.

The Career Press, Inc.
220 West Parkway, Unit 12
Pompton Plains, NJ 07444
www.careerpress.com
www.newpagebooks.com

Library of Congress Cataloging-in-Publication Data

CIP Data Available Upon Request.

Dedication

I want to dedicate this book to Alisa, who is the love of my life. For your presence in my life and in my heart, and for holding an energy that enables us to live "heaven on earth" while on this planet together.

Acknowledgments

My deepest thanks to Alisa Logan, who shared the urgency for this material to be made available now, and who has been by my side though the whole process of writing this book. It would not have been completed without her support. With her amazing expertise she was able to bring so much to the completion process of this channeled material.

My heartfelt thanks to my agent, Laurie Harper, for once again offering your expertise, support, trust, understanding, and friendship.

My love and appreciation to Reid Kruger of Waterbury Music and Sound for the recording and editing of all the material for this book, for the ease in which you share your expertise, and for the spark of joy you bring to our connection and friendship.

I want to acknowledge my daughter, Lisa Glynn, for being such a magnificent gift in my life, and for the work she has done with the diagrams and drawings for this book. I witness you and your journey, my darling girl, with my deepest love and respect for you.

A special thank you to Don Kelly for all your support and your commitment to do the final editing of this book.

To my dearest and most treasured friends, Jo Bray, Lorelee Wederstrom, Ruth Palmer, Susan Arthur, Anne Westfield, Sally Kerwin, and Efren Solanas, who are part of my family. Thank you for all of your love, support, and encouragement along the way.

My gratitude and special thanks to the Frequencies of Brilliance practitioners in Minnesota who have held such a loving space around this book as it was undertaken and completed; your love has made a tremendous impact on me. My deepest gratitude to all the practitioners, teachers, and students who hold me with so much love on my mission to bring the Pleiadian message to the world.

And I end with all my love to my four granddaughters, Cienna, Bailee, Sailor, and Evie, for all the joy and celebration you bring to my heart.

Contents

Introduction   **9**

Introduction From the Pleiadians   **13**

Chapter 1
Redefining Your Relationship to Your Human Self:
Being Human/Being Sacred   17

Chapter 2
Conscious Choice and Pre-Agreements   24

Chapter 3
Activating Your Crystalline Structure   35

Chapter 4
Activating Your Telepathic Communication and
Telepathic Communion   48

Chapter 5
Harnessing the Energy of the Earth's Natural Forces:
Sacred Communion With Nature   60

Chapter 6
Aligning to Your Mission, Fulfilling Your Destiny   74

Chapter 7
Building Your Telepathic Communion With   84
Life Force Groups

Chapter 8
Crop Circles   95

Chapter 9
The Sacred Matrix   107

Chapter 10
Activating Your Command Energy:
Conscious Choice to Activate Your Energetic Portals   118

Chapter 11
Working With Your Command Energy and the
Earth's Natural Energies: Creating Energetic Alliances   130

Chapter 12
Aligning to Your Sacred Flow, Re-United to Your Place   145

Appendix A
Questions and Answers   **157**

Appendix B
Ongoing Work with Christine   **182**

Index   **187**

About the Author   **191**

Introduction

I write this book with immense love and appreciation for all that the Pleiadians have given me throughout the last 27 years. Contemplating this second book was daunting, but I realized that this material and its transformational initiations were going to bring significant change to many lives. This book offers a tremendous amount of support and understanding with which you can navigate yourself along your own path at this amazing time on the earth plane. I wrote this book because of the magnitude of information that was part of my mission to bring to you.

I am grateful now for all that I have been given during this undertaking. I could not have imagined my journey when I once again opened up to the Pleiadians' beauty, love, and impeccable ability to bring a sacred synergy through these amazing initiations for self-empowerment. I am in awe of their ability to bring forward their pure essence within the processes for all human beings. They are completely committed to you.

I have undergone enormous personal transformation as I brought in the material for this book. More accurately, I met the true beauty of my Self. I experienced aspects of my unlimited Self that were not previously revealed to me, and within this, the simple truth and clarity of the unlimited aspect of my Self within the moment.

This whole process has allowed me to become closer to the Pleiadians within a new dimensional setting, to step forward and deeply appreciate them from a new perspective. The level of love that I have been able to experience with them has transformed my heart.

I know that I am not the same as I was before I started writing this book. I questioned why this introduction had to be the piece that was written last, but I now understand. There was no way that I could fully comprehend the material in this book before writing it. I thought I could, but in retrospect I really had no understanding of what energies of light this book would hold or just how much impact it would have on me.

The energies held within this book are transformational and timely. The book is designed to move you to sacred "Principles for Living" so that you can once more re-align with the rest of the Universe by reuniting with your sacred aspects.

The initiation processes bring truths for you to live by. A series of understandings are revealed to you so that you can live within these principles through a natural re-alignment with your Self and a metamorphosis within your cells when you activate the frequencies that carry the "Principles for Living."

As human beings you are capable of birthing aspects of this New Dawning energy that carry the essence of these Principles for Living, because the veils have lifted on the earth plane. Since 12/12/12, dimensional openings have naturally occurred on the planet, giving all of you opportunities to rejoin the Collective Consciousness.

As I wrote this book, I had many moments in which I was transported into different realities of truth and then held in a loving embrace. At those times, I went through my own metamorphosis within my cells. These were extraordinary, exhilarating experiences. I understand now that this is and always has been present alongside the third-dimensional illusion of the earth plane. I am in celebration of my Self and can fully appreciate all that I have been through on my journey as a human being, and all that I have experienced and created for my learning process.

I know that my rebirth has taken place, bringing me into alignment with the rest of the Universe. I know that now I can just Be. Finally, I have come to a resting place at which I can begin the rest of my life. I use the term "resting place," which may sound like the end of my life, but it is really just the beginning!

What does this mean? I have stepped outside the illusion of this earth plane and anchored there. I know that my human aspect has let go of certain third-dimensional attachments, and this has opened up the possibility of a new relationship between my human aspect and my divine aspect. A level of separation has ended within me. I can now move into a more unlimited experience of Being and receive what is naturally mine, which is abundance on all levels.

I am aware of a new physical strength within my body, and I can somehow perceive life from a very different angle. Writing about my process is helping me to define *what* it is that I am now and *where* it is that I am now. It's almost as though I was looking at the world one way and then was turned to experience me, the world, and the Universe from a different viewpoint.

It is fascinating to me how quickly my reality changed. I know it has taken many different moments in time for me to come to this place, and there are many turning points still ahead of me. I don't need to be anywhere but here in my current-awareness experience. I move to my next step, however it presents itself, and I am completely dedicated to my path and my mission, wherever it takes me. I am committed to this moment in time, appreciating this moment, breathing and willing in my continual unfolding. This journey becomes a simple process of allowing myself to Be.

What goes hand-in-hand and feels important to share is that I am really unattached to *your* process. What I mean is I am unattached to what you choose to do and the steps you choose to take toward your Self. That is really your business, not mine. I hold doorways open for you to step through, and then it is up to you to walk through these open doorways. Being unattached allows me to hold a very large space for each one of you with a tremendous amount of love without judgment. Through my detachment I can bring all of myself forward, holding the fullest space of love for you. Understand that I am committed to working with you energetically as you initiate. You only need to call my energy forward and I will be with you, assisting you in your integration of the material, and holding a space for your awakening.

Please be aware that the Pleiadian energy I channel is very strong, as it is a natural part of my aspect and connection to the Pleiadians. They bring the energy through me to you in the way you need it in the moment; it may not be what you want, but what you need for your next step.

How to Use This Book

It feels important to review how you are going to work through this book. There are 27 audio files for you to access and work with, which are at the end of most chapters throughout the book. You can access these audio files on the Internet, where you will be able to download them for free using a code that is included at the back of the book.

Each audio file holds a channeled initiation for you, and each initiation is multi-dimensional in nature. This means you can listen to it unlimited times;

each time you will have a different journey experience and you will birth into another level of your Self.

It is important for you to read each chapter in sequence because the energies build as you move through the book. Take your time with each chapter and know that you can read each chapter and listen to each audio file more than one time. You will probably need to take more than one journey of each audio file. This is a common experience.

Also know that within many chapters there is more than one audio file. Some chapters have three or four. It is important to listen to them in the order they are given.

I want to honor you for this next step you are taking toward your Self. Know that the whole Universe witnesses you as you move forward on this journey!

With love and blessings,
Christine

Introduction From the Pleiadians

Beloved Ones,

There is a great power birthing and rising in your world, opening for you a new perception that is taking you in a new direction. You are being gently guided from one world to another. And this is your process of purpose for this lifetime, bringing you into an alignment with Truth. There is a revelation taking place before you, and at the same time within you. What a gift you are within this transformation process! You are an integral part of the transformational experience now in this "New Dawning."

We are here to assist you by bringing information so that you gain a deeper understanding of the process that is taking place on your earth plane. With this clarity you can begin to step forward into your own birthing process. You can re-claim your Self through conscious choice and remember your pre-agreements.

You see, you are to play a major role in the transformation on your planet. There is a master design and you are a woven part of it. As you awaken you will assist in a continual birthing process on your earth plane by holding energetic spaces, creating energetic grids, and helping anchor new light frequencies onto the earth plane. When you say yes to your pre-agreements and take up your role, you are able to work with the earth's energy.

This time on your planet is like no other because it allows you through conscious choice to re-align your Self to the origin of your light consciousness.

The new dimensional alignments taking place within your earth plane are a part of the New Dawning energy. They are here for you to utilize for your own birthing process. Because of your plan that you set in place, to be activated and realized now, you are experiencing a deep understanding of who you are within the greater plan. A unique timing mechanism has been set in motion to reveal many truths to you.

Your world within planet Earth is moving back into alignment with the rest of the Universe. This is like a curtain lifting on a stage, revealing an entirely new panorama. You belong within this new setting. You will begin to recognize and remember your place on this magical stage. You will begin to learn to use your natural gifts within you and once more dance within the Universe.

The understandings that will be revealed to you will give you a new clarity about who you are in your natural brilliance. You will remember your place within the Universal Consciousness, and you can begin to experience a unity of love with all life force within the universe.

You are a part of this "life force" so this process of re-birth especially involves a re-uniting with Self. When we talk about Self it includes two parts of you—the divine aspect and the human aspect. You are experiencing a transformation with the relationship with your human aspect. This is essential because the separation between divine and human that has existed for lifetimes within you must end so you can move forward into your enlightenment process, and once more take your place within the Collective Consciousness.

Through this re-awakening you can begin to have a direct, conscious experience of divine love, and remember your divine plan. Your unique frequency of consciousness has an important place within the grand plan.

We are here at this time to hold energetic doorways open for you, to give you access to this understanding and begin to utilize your newly found natural gifts within you. We welcome you and honor you for all that you have experienced on your journey so far in this lifetime.

This clarity will enable you to open doors. These are your doorways that have been waiting for you. The doorways themselves hold the energetic memory codes that belong to you. They allow you to remember your pre-agreements to be here on this earth plane at this time.

The activation of your personal codes will link you into the new grid lines that have activated on your planet, allowing you to naturally flow and become a part of the multi-dimensional birthing of the new consciousness; a mutual birthing of consciousness.

Your light that births from the activation of your personal codes will re-define your energies so you will be able to move forward with a transformed sense of yourself. You re-align to Truth, and are able to remember what was always going to take place within you and the earth plane at this time. As you consciously open up to this alignment, you begin to hold an awakening energy within your cells and energetic field. You are a gift to the world.

As you open into this experience of remembering you begin to naturally activate a series of re-alignments, bringing you back into many dimensional aspects of your light Self, opening you into a re-union with the Universal Consciousness. This whole journey is about re-aligning to a natural state of your own energetic flow that exists as a part of the Universal Consciousness.

It is essential that you consciously choose to participate in your role. This allows a much more powerful aspect of your energy to anchor on your planet Earth. As you open into this energy there is an automatic shift within your system. The cells in your body begin a metamorphosis.

Since 11/11/11 your cells have begun to birth a new crystalline re-structuring to enable you to hold the expanded energies of Self. Your physical body will begin to be capable of holding your full light. Up until now your aspect of light has been held outside your physical body because you did not have the capacity for containing the full energy of Self. This is part of the physical metamorphosis that is taking place within your cells right now.

Your crystalline structure has anchored into your body. Now it needs to be activated. We bring to you the activation processes for your crystalline structure. Ultimately this will allow a re-activation of your telepathic center within your brain, giving you access to a sacred communion with the Collective Consciousness, to all life force within the Universe.

This expanded communion will be beyond anything that you can imagine with your ego mind. It will be a communion through the heart and will bring a birthing of a simple and powerful joy that will transform all cells within your being. This outrageous joy will bring waves of transformational light within your energetic field, creating an activation of the sacred codes within your body. You will begin to vibrate in an alignment to the earth's energy.

These sacred energetic codes have been in place. YOU have set them in place for YOU to activate and receive now. The codes activate through a series of sacred sounds. Part of our role is to provide you with these sacred sounds. As you transmit the sounds, your unique frequency will birth. Your cells will respond to your frequency birthing codes, and these codes activate a Truth within you. You will recognize the energetic of this Truth. You will remember.

Know that you are ready to receive these transforming codes. They bring you into a new alignment to your spiritual gifts, activating a remembering of your natural divine link to your place within the Universal Consciousness.

The energies on the earth plane are also changing dramatically. Because of the birthing of the new dimensional energies the natural forces on your planet are coming into a new state of consciousness. This means that the earth itself is holding a new essence, a deeper ability to work with each one of you, playing the important role of integrator for you within your birthing process.

It is important that you utilize these new connections consciously. An important alliance is created through this mutual birthing process. You must recognize and acknowledge this. As you move toward this exchange between you and the natural forces there is an energetic flow that can weave between you, which opens doorways between you, building a sacred alliance.

You are going to need to build this sacred alliance as the earth changes begin to accelerate. The developing union will support you moving with the flowing changes, and help you to stay in balance with each dimensional shift as it unfolds. The developing relationship will also enable you to fulfill an aspect of your role in holding energetic vortex positions on the earth plane to assist in the dimensional transformation of your planet.

Our role right now is to first bring you the information so you can begin to understand and remember. Then we hold a series of energetic platforms that act like a mirror for you to be able to re-align back to your energy for your awakening. We hold the energetic mirror that reflects your essence. We do not bring our own energies forward to interfere with your process. This process is all about you and the journey that you have pre-agreed to be a part of. We have made pre-agreements to support you in this way as part of OUR journey. We witness you. We cannot interfere with your energies in any way.

There is a series of awakenings that need to take place within you, a gradual process in increments of your energetic light. Each part of the process builds on the previous. The birthing of a light within you moves into each physical cell of your body. It holds your unique spiritual signature. We rejoice with each new ray of light that you receive back to your self, and welcome your newly birthed state with each step that you take.

We bring you the light initiations to help you navigate these changing times and to assist you in your awakening. We offer a perspective of this time on your planet to empower you in your birthing process, in the Earth's birthing process, and to recognize you as you take your place within the Universal Consciousness. We hold the space for you to activate your pre-agreement. We are waiting for you.

Your time has come for self-mastery.

This is what you have come here to do.

Open up your eyes...see your Self; be seen.

Open up your heart...receive your Self with love; be received with love.

The new frequencies of light and sound that are now bathing the planet are awakening you to the remembrance of and reconnection of your true Self.

We celebrate you!

Blessings,
The Pleiadians

1

Redefining Your Relationship to Your Human Self: Being Human/Being Sacred

You hold the sacred design of your New Dawning pattern within you. Your unique design is a part of the collective energy, ready to birth through your cells. It is going to require your conscious participation, meaning that you claim your Self now through this sacred design. This is the pre-agreement that you made, to come and do this now.

The new dimensional energies anchoring onto the planet support, hold, and align with you, so you are able to move away from the third-dimensional separation within you. It's like breaking the mold that has held you in place for lifetimes. This is part of a grace given to you in the New Dawning, designed to make it easier for you to open into this new relationship, this new way of being with your Self.

The new fourth/fifth-dimensional energies that are birthing onto the planet allow you to take your next step in building a new relationship with your Self. It allows you appreciation for your human element, honoring yourself for all that you have gone through on this journey so far on this planet, and for every experience you have created for your Self.

An important part of your learning process is to know and understand your human vulnerabilities so you can appreciate and support yourself on this journey. It is essential that you bring *all* parts of your Self on this journey of transformation. In order to do this you must be able to love all aspects of your Self, and embrace all parts of your vulnerability.

Your human aspect has another role to play during this New Dawning. Its third-dimensional role is almost complete, and its new fourth/fifth-dimensional role involves being part of a working union with your divine spiritual aspect, with all parts of your Self consciously flowing together, taking steps toward home.

Many of you have an internal separation with yourselves based on self-judgment and self-condemnation for things you've done, the experiences you have lived, and the choices you have made or not made. You have a list of things that you have held against yourselves, and yet you have chosen to have this human experience.

The Pleiadians continue to remind us that everyone is "perfectly imperfect" as human beings. Yet, the lie is that, in order to be enlightened, you have to be perfect. Really, all you have to do to become enlightened is end the separation inside your Self and accept your Self in your "perfectly imperfect" state. You cannot move into enlightenment while you are separated with your Self. You need to celebrate your humanness; remember that you came to the earth plane to have a human experience.

A big component of this shift (the Pleiadians say "the most important part") is the process of self-acceptance in which you move into a practice of self-love. This will come automatically when the fourth/fifth-dimensional energies anchor onto the earth plane; however, right now there is still a third-dimensional illusion operating on the earth plane.

As you transform, your spiritual aspect can evolve because your internal separation ends. This transformation will birth within you a sense of peace and stability, and bring you back into re-alignment with a fourth/fifth-dimensional relationship with your Self. You will become a witness to the third-dimensional drama on this earth plane rather than being a part of it. It is time to come full circle, back to your Self. You'll be amazed how quickly your life will unfold once you begin unraveling what is inside.

As a human being you tend to put your attention toward distractions. You move your energy outside of your Self. It is challenging to feel the human element within your Self, to feel your vulnerability, to explore what is inside of you.

It is important to understand the process of your creation. When you need to learn something your higher divine aspect creates a series of situations within your world as a way for you to have an experience. This enables you to take another step toward a better understanding of your human vulnerabilities. Sometimes a situation is created so that you have another opportunity to work through an issue that you did not deal with in previous experiences.

You don't interpret it that way when you are in your human aspect, when you're in the illusion, but the truth is, everything that comes toward you is mirroring what's already inside of you, all that you have not been able to work through. By owning your creation, you begin to deal with the feelings inside that arose from the situation.

As you are willing to bring your awareness right into the center of the feeling that is inside of you, you breathe into the feeling, almost as though you're drowning in the experience. Then the feeling can leave the body. The situation will also be able to leave because it is no longer required. Your healing is complete; the issue has released.

This is the recipe for dealing with the issues inside of you. Realize that you can no longer be a victim in your life. This is your key piece to the transformation of your separation elements. What is going on in each person's life is each person's creation, so that they can transform. This birthing process is not easy, but you create what you need in each moment. It might be uncomfortable, traumatic, or dramatic, and it might cause chaos inside of you, but it is all coming as a gift.

Within the New Dawning energy there is support for you to own where you are in your path right now. Through the action of your Conscious Choice, you are enabling yourself to align to your spiritual aspect. As you consciously own your creation, and open to the feelings that are being provoked, a transformational process will begin to take place. This is you beginning to consciously work in alignment with your divine Self, your creator Self. This re-union will begin to propel you forward on your path, and you will be able to move differently in your world as you flow in alignment with your destiny pathway.

It all comes down to two elements: fear and love. When disturbing feelings come up, and you study what you're holding against yourself, you'll be amazed. Equally amazing is how fast your life will transform. It's unbelievably magical how quickly you can change and turn things around in your life with this process. I encourage you to open up to your life and be willing to own your creation. Be willing to feel what is in front of you. The question to ask your self is, "What is the lesson in front of me right now?"

Give yourself permission to remember, to make mistakes. You do not need to be perfect. Take joy in humanness, remove yourself from the cross, hold yourself in love and understanding, and breathe into your cells. Align with your sacred heart; your heart is the connection between spirit and human. Bring in the sun; the sun is the light of you. Honor yourself for every slip on the journey and hold every aspect of your experience with love and compassion. Each cell resonates and resurrects with this glorious experience of ending separation.

This process of ending your internal separation touches my heart deeply. The journey I took to end the separation was a powerful process. I was on a conscious path of awakening, committed to my journey and my mission, knowing that an important part of my ongoing unfolding involved working on my Self. I shared my meeting with Jesus in an earlier book. It was during this discourse with Jesus that he showed me how I had put myself up on a cross with tremendous self-condemnation. I was shocked and yet I knew what he said was true. He also said that *I had put myself up on that cross* and I was the only one who could take me off. He told me I had come here to resurrect myself in this lifetime.

As I spent time with this information I discovered a huge internal separation within me, and my next step was introspection, self-examination for all the things I was holding against myself. Each day I would take one item from my long list and hold myself, reminding myself I was "perfectly imperfect" and that I came here to learn through my mistakes. I would remind myself that I was not responsible for anyone else's experience. As I did this I could feel that huge, tight ball inside of me slightly loosen.

I could feel the importance of working toward holding myself with love and compassion for all that I had suffered within the experience I was working on. Each moment that I was able to successfully hold myself with love and compassion was accumulative. I didn't know how long this process was going to take; I just committed to learning about me, my vulnerabilities, and my fears.

One day as I completed a moment of holding myself, an amazing thing happened. There was an explosion of light and Mother Mary was standing beside me. Behind me my cross was burning. In that moment my internal ball of twine collapsed, and the separation ended inside me. I was filled with the glorious truth of my life, knowing that everyone had played their parts perfectly so I could have my learning experiences. I was filled with a joy and exhilaration beyond anything I had ever experienced. The beauty of that moment is still with me, and the truth of that moment transformed me and the way that I live each moment of every day.

I didn't need to work down my whole list as I had imagined. I just had to reach a point for that tight ball of twine to loosen, and then I was able to transform and liberate myself from the separation within, and my cross burned behind me.

This birthing process was such a glorious moment, and it continues to unfold me, even now, years later. The truth doesn't leave you; when you get to that pure truth it continues to evolve through you. There is a tremendous love that began to naturally birth through every one of my cells, opening me up to a powerful self-healing process. This was a natural result of my transformation.

I encourage each one of you to begin your list, to open to the next step of your journey. There is no greater reason to do this than self-love. Take a breath. Claim your Self and your humanity. It makes all things possible. Allow all experiences as learning experiences. Allow everything else in your life to be, to just rest.

After Your Separation Has Healed, What Next?

When you have healed the third-dimensional separation within you, you will have evolved into a stable alignment to the fourth/fifth-dimensional realm. At times you will need to revisit the third dimension to complete the healing within your humanness, and this is okay. As you evolve you will consciously open to your ongoing learning process. No longer a victim, you will embrace whatever experiences come your way.

Most important, your transformation will allow you to fulfill your mission by working in alignment with the natural forces on planet Earth and expand into a more conscious working relationship with the spiritual realms on a daily level. A direct alignment into the sacred heart consciousness creates the sacred connection between your humanness and your divine aspect. This enables you to move differently in the world and have a different experience with your Self and other human beings. You begin to experience the truth of Oneness.

Your individual transformational journey will support the earth plane in its unfolding, because when you end your internal separation, your abilities expand to help anchor the transformation of human consciousness. This anchoring within the earth plane plays a major role in assisting others to make their own transformation journeys.

You become the gift just by being on the earth plane and carrying the element of re-union within you. You become a natural transmitter of the love you have become. It is important that *now* is the time for you to take your steps forward to fulfill this aspect of your mission.

There are many life force groups within the Universe. Human beings are the only life force group within the whole Universe still operating within the third-dimensional illusion. Because of the separation that exists within the human element it is challenging for you to trust each other, fully let go, and open your hearts to each other.

Initially, you are going to find it easier to open up to other life force groups within your planet, such as the plant kingdom, the mineral kingdom, and the animal kingdom, In addition, you will open to other life force groups outside your planet, such as all aspects of the spiritual realms, the alien energies, and all other life force within the Universe. All of these have a consciousness that can support you right now in your integration and birthing process. It is important to seek out their support and know you are not alone in this aspect of your journey. The support of Mother Mary, the Pleiadians, the Angels, Sai Baba, Jesus, and many Light beings has been an integral part of my resurrection process. It was never intended that we complete this journey of self-resurrection alone!

The time will come when the human race will need to open up and receive each other in a loving union. Just like the ball of twine that I described in my resurrection process, there will be a moment when the collective energy of many of us will manifest this transformation and the separation will collapse. Then the truth of this interconnection that exists between us and the God essence will be revealed. This time will come naturally as we begin to unfold. This truth will liberate you and then naturally extend out to meet other humans through your heart center. As all separation ends, our hearts will meet within the Oneness on the fifth-dimensional level.

As our crystalline structures birth within each one of us and our crystalline energies are activated, the union with all human beings becomes a possibility. The common element among all unique crystalline structures is the God consciousness. It is this element that links us and allows you to experience Oneness with all life force within the Universe, including all human beings. This is a glorious time of true re-union of soul groups. Now is the time for you to begin opening toward this mutual life force that we share with all human beings. The end of separation between all human beings has to start with you.

There will come a time on Earth when the third-dimensional illusion will no longer exist here. You don't have to wait long for this; the actual third-dimensional energy can leave your world now. You can choose to move through these pieces very quickly, because there's a huge new supportive energy on the planet.

There are some difficult times coming on the earth plane and there will be many challenges. Your transformation process to end your separation will support you during challenging times. It will help you stay out of the human drama and experience clarity and connection with the flow of your intuition. You will be able to consciously move with the birthing energies of the changes as they come. You can consciously meet this glorious time and open up to your place in it.

Your first step right now is to birth your Self consciously and be willing to meet all aspects of your vulnerability. Find your sacred connections. This is where "all" that is inside of you and your connection to the universe lies.

Sit and be with your Self. When you are ready, take this step. I truly hold that space for you.

~~~

Beloved Ones,

We greet you; we honor you and the journey you have chosen to take on this earth plane. We honor your human journey, and the steps you take toward your resurrection process. We remind you of your divine alliance to all other human beings on your planet, and the importance to see how each human being is doing the best they can within their own experience. We witness each person in that experience, honoring how they need to be within the choices that they make for themselves in each moment. It's about not interfering in another's way, understanding that they need this experience and will do what they need to do in their own time. This is a true loving action, not trying to fix anything for them. Nothing needs to be fixed.

You need to witness the drama around you but not become part of that drama. Make a choice to focus on what you have created around you. Open to the moment of learning and feel what is here for you to understand within your creation. Hold your Self with love in this moment.

We remind you of the intensification of the third-dimensional illusion on your earth plane. Don't get caught up in it. Know that through your sacred heart there is stillness, a peace, and truth that will be revealed. Begin with the Conscious Choice to align more and more within your sacred heart. You can do this for yourself and make a huge difference, to yourself and also to anchor this energy for the planet and for all human kind.

We love and support you in this. Reach out to us. Call us forward for support in all ways. It is the time.

Blessings,
The Pleiadians

~~~

2

Conscious Choice and Pre-Agreements

In this New Dawning, the dimensional energies on the earth plane have changed, and will continue to expand and change. The Earth is going through a metamorphosis, and human beings are going through great physical and spiritual transformation. An important and exciting next step is to change the way you work with your personal power. In the past, you played a passive role, sitting back and waiting for experiences to come to you. Now in this New Dawning, the time has come for you to open up through the action of Conscious Choice, to utilize your personal power.

In the very movement of choosing you are aligned to the natural flow of your personal power. This begins a journey, re-aligning to your original aspect as a "Being of Light," back into your place among the Collective Consciousness within the Universe.

This journey is about you taking back your power and your responsibility for being here on this earth plane and living out your truth and authenticity. The dimensional shift within the earth plane has created a "lifting of the veils" to bring you new opportunities in which you can consciously relate to and interact with aspects of your divine Self. This new dimensional energy has re-opened a pathway for you to journey within a different energetic framework, within yourself, on the earth plane. The new pathway helps you remember your mission and reconnect to sacred parts of your Self. This new pathway allows you to re-align back into the sacred Principles for Living, joining the rest of the Universe through these sacred principles. These principles hold a high frequency of love, allowing you to return to divine aspects of your Self, helping your human aspect move consciously into a fourth-dimensional experience of truth and leaving third-dimensional drama behind. The energies within these Principles for Living carry the energy of Oneness, so your human aspect naturally begins to align into a state of union with the sacred aspect of your Self.

Your Active Blueprint

There is a grand plan leading you step by step to the completion of these changing times. An aspect of the plan has been created by you and for you to align to your blueprint through Conscious Choice when the time is right for you. And for many of you, the time is now. This is an exciting next step that will propel you forward toward your own destiny!

I liken this plan to a map that unites you to your own unique framework of energy within the whole of the Collective Consciousness. This map will allow you to understand and connect to, align with, and witness the overview of Self within the Collective Consciousness at this time. During your journey this map brings to you a deeper understanding of the important part you play now during these Earth changes. This will support you in consciously participating within your role by bringing a clarity in which you can align to the sacred Principles for Living that exist within the Universal Consciousness.

I have been working with my own aspect of this map for many years and it has brought me into an accelerated awakened state in order to complete my first mission blueprint. As I began to understand my place within the Collective energies I was able to more fully step forward into my power and align with these sacred principles that exist within the Universe. Each one of you holds the energy of these principles within your cells. They begin to activate as you awaken and align to your blueprints. For example, I previously shared the story of beginning my second mission blueprint for this lifetime in my last book.

Each one of you created your "blueprint" before you came on to this earth plane. A blueprint is like an active pathway that contains your unique, divine signature, aligning you to your mission here. You have created your blueprint that contains your individual mission, and this energy of your blueprint is what moves you toward fulfilling your mission. Your Sacred Consciousness is woven throughout your blueprint, aligning you directly with your place within the Collective Consciousness. You cannot be on this earth plane without a current active blueprint.

You activate this natural alignment to your blueprint, to what you have pre-chosen for yourself at this time, by your Conscious Choice. For lifetimes your ego mind has controlled your movements. With the New Dawning energy, a stronger current of truth moves you forward, like a current in a river, weaving you into the light of your divine connection. The simple action of you making a *Conscious Choice* to call forward your alignment to your blueprint is all you need to do. This is like a key re-opening the door to your pathway.

By utilizing your Conscious Choice, you are able to return to your natural birthright of opportunity, activating the energies of the Principles for Living that are held within the cells of your body. In doing so, you begin to create an impact within the Universal Consciousness because you align energetically with the Universe as these Living Principles are activated. It is as though you become a vibrating frequency of light that can resonate within the Universe. You begin to take your place!

Why Does Your Action of Conscious Choice Create This Impact?

When you activate your Conscious Choice, your energetic imprint is activated throughout the Universal Grid, which allows an expansion of your natural place there. This wave of your imprint energy creates a brightness of your light, completing another aspect of Self within the grid. You begin to anchor more into home. Your divine signature of light begins to expand and interact with all life force within the Universe; this essence of your light affects the balance within the Collective Consciousness and within the Universe. Know that the moment you move through a Conscious Choice action for the Principles for Living, energy begins to rebirth through you.

The Universal Grid is like a huge jigsaw puzzle. You have your unique piece to fit in the puzzle. No other energy has this piece. Each time you activate your Conscious Choice your piece of the puzzle begins to vibrate, to come alive, so your unique frequency of light can begin to fulfill the role within the collective energies of this energetic grid. You make the difference. As you work with your Conscious Choice, your place within the Universal Grid begins to hold multifaceted aspects of your collective sacred energies. As these sacred aspects birth, they can assist you, work with you, and help you fulfill your mission.

Each time you open into your Conscious Choice action here on the earth plane, further birthing connections are made to your place within the Universal Grid. Your energetic grid pathway expands dimensionally throughout the cells of your body, activating an awakening process. The cells in your body begin to vibrate to your frequency of home, and there is a transformational process that takes place within your physical body, aligning to the vibration of love that exists within your place on the Universal Grid. Your cells are tuned like a radio to this frequency of love that exists within your place on this grid. Each time you work through a Conscious Choice action you align another level to this frequency of love and move another step toward home.

The changing frequency within your body supports the transformation of the planet. Your assistance in the anchoring of these new dimensional states on our earth plane is important because your unique energies are much more potent than any work the Pleiadians do. When you begin to activate pre-agreement energies, the essence, result, and overall dynamic is much more powerful within the Collective Consciousness. You can make a significant impact through the completion of your pre-agreements.

As you move into being in the moment, the cells in your body adjust and align themselves to this new dimensional level, and a new consciousness of Self can birth. You have a choice *in each moment* to open to another part of your Self. Your cells are waiting for you to align to any given moment. When you do this, you move out of separation and into a multi-dimensional expression of that moment. This creates an unlimited form, because you move out of the third dimension and into a fifth-dimensional aspect of that moment. The audio file recommended later in this chapter will introduce you to a process that opens into these opportunities within the moment.

Time does not exist, so within that one moment of activating your Conscious Choice you are expanded into an unlimited experience of Being, into what is being fully revealed. Within this timelessness there are many aspects of space, and there are no limitations. You will experience a freedom of Being as you step forward into your experiences of the moment.

Your Conscious Choice Group Process

The Pleiadians bring a process that will enable each one of you to move into another level of your awakening with each other, to move into a state of non-separation with your Self and each other.

A part of this process is to bring forward your Conscious Choice energy by participating within a circle of two or more people. The smallest gathering of two people can place four chairs or cushions in a position to create the energy of a circle. The largest gathering can hold an unlimited amount of people or a series of circles, depending on the space.

Sit in a circle with no agenda. Just Be. Watch the ego mind trying to create a structure so it can participate: *What about playing music before we start, or in the background? Can we put candles and crystals in the center of the circle? Can we burn incense? Can we share experiences at the end?* The ego will always make comments and ask questions to make this more complex than it is.

As you take your place within the circle (and everyone takes their place in this way without ego), the circle energy can access a natural portal that allows you to receive your Selves in a new dimensional space of being. This portal activates when two or more people pre-agree to sit in a circle with no agenda and are open to being together for a higher purpose than the ego.

When this gathering takes place it allows a fourth/fifth-dimensional anchoring to open within your circle. At the same time, it births new energetic patterns within the earth plane, patterns of new dimensional light that support this transitional time on the earth plane.

You are being called forward to sit in as many circles as possible at this time. This process will also help you create a transformed alignment within your energetic field for a more expanded birthing of your light energies and acceleration of your awakening. The more you are willing to sit in these conscious circles the more will be revealed to you for your awakening. When you choose this avenue of experience, the portals that open within your circles bring a new dawning of consciousness to you. These portals hold the alignments to the Principles for Living and you open into the knowledge and understanding by linking into a Universal vortex. You choose connection, Oneness, truth, re-alignment, re-union, and remembering. The energies coming on to the planet will lift many veils. It is up to you how you choose to receive yourself now.

You cannot imagine how transformative it is when a group of human beings comes together just to Be, with no human agenda, within a circle, choosing something other than third-dimensional experience.

~~~

My Beloved Ones,

You are being asked at this time to open up and live through your heart center. It is through the heart that you will begin to understand your true path and will be able to understand this new perspective of living by being. It's through the heart that you will come into a realization of truth—truth about what is important in your lives.

You will turn toward each other with a new understanding of love. When we talk about love we talk about authenticity and integrity of action with yourself, and the action that you bring to each other, letting go of the petty thoughts of the ego mind that create separation. The time has gone to be hanging onto old rivalries, old hurts, and big ego.

There is no competition here, only a moving together and a sharing of love; moving together in consciousness, as one wave in motion. The time has come to let go of the separation, because in truth, outside the ego it does not exist. Find others like you who are prepared to move with this wave of connection. Build your alliances and bring your unique consciousness to the group connection. Honor the differences that you bring, open up your hearts, and join as one.

With the coming times you will need these connections. Together, you form a strong wave of light that will make a huge difference on your planet. Come together in circles, and allow the energy of your circle to expand and grow in consciousness. It is important to allow your circle to grow in numbers. Don't close your circle off to others; greet each newcomer as a precious aspect of the light that brings a unique frequency to your circle energy.

Remember that you are human, and that you are not perfect so mistakes will be made. Forgive yourselves as you take your steps forward and begin this alliance with each other. Open to forgiveness of yourself, and forgiveness of others. Let go and open to this great opportunity that is before you!

With much love,
The Pleiadians

~~~

Activating Your Conscious Choice
Audio file: Chapter 2
Audio file #1

Today you are being asked to hold your heart and allow the birthing of a new connection within your Self, saying, *Yes, I am willing to accept this letting go and open to this new alignment for myself.* Each choice you make now will create powerful change within you and within your cells. Make a choice and then simply *let go.* Trust your flow. Do not try to control your process. Adjustments will be made through your energetic field and this will bring you an adjusted perception of your world. This is instantaneously activated through your cells, energetic field, and consciousness.

Breathe and let go. There will be change within you and a new alignment within your consciousness.

Pre-Agreements

With the changing of your consciousness you begin to play a new role. Part of this new role is to call forth the pre-agreements that you set in place to support you at this time in your evolution. Calling pre-agreements into action opens up a destiny pathway that you set in place. It activates energetic alignments within you to aspects of your sacred Self, and aligns you to a higher frequency of flow.

Through Conscious Choice you claim your birthright to work with energetic alliances within the Universe, and in doing so you begin to align back to your sacred role within the Collective Consciousness. You open into a working relationship with these energetic alliances.

The most significant pre-agreement you made was saying yes to being here at this time on the planet, playing your role, and fulfilling your mission during this transformational time. It is powerful to affirm this commitment, and as you confirm this Truth, you create another turn in the wheel for yourself. By reaffirming this, you set in motion a next step, empowering your Self to receive another aspect of Self. You begin to step into a fuller role within your path. As you do this, other dimensional doors on your path open.

Allow the Universe to witness you and see how your path accelerates when you do this. It's about launching your Self in a new conscious way.

There are many pre-agreements that you created, and many of them are now ready to be activated by you. All of these pre-agreements were put into place so that you would have the support you need at this time to fulfill your mission here on this earth plane. You may not remember what these pre-agreement entail or even with whom they are with. It is unimportant. Just trust yourself enough to know that you have set these in place in order to receive what you are going to need now and through the coming times.

Through the activation of your pre-agreement connections within the other dimensional realms you are able to launch yourself forward on a new conscious path. You cannot make this part of your journey alone. The path is designed for you to unfold with this support. This next aspect of your journey holds a strong loving component of union with other beings.

This learning process of working with others through your heart is new for you. These connections are really a natural part of you, and now is the time for you to open into this expanded experience of your Self within a multi-dimensional union and your essence as a spiritual being within these partnerships. You have free will as a human being, so these energetic alliances cannot come forward and support you without you activating them through your Conscious Choice.

Each of you has different alliances. Some of you have pre-agreements with the Spiritual realms: the Angels, Light beings, and Masters. Some of you have pre-agreements with specific energies, such as Mother Mary, Jesus, Sai Baba, Buddha, Quan Yen, and other alliance Beings. Some of you have your pre-agreements with the Galactic council, Pleiadians, and other Star energies.

You may be working with a certain group of energies, or one particular energy. As you activate your pre-agreements you may find a very different group coming forward to assist you. It may be the time for new alliances to be here for you at this pivotal time, and it may be that you have a destiny to complete your projects with this different group of energetic forces.

I know as human beings you become attached to certain energies supporting you. Maybe some of you have been working with the same guides or individual masters for some time on your path. However, within the changes that are here, many of you will be ready for new support systems. You need to trust and be open to these new alliances. As you consciously align you are able to turn a corner, opening to another dimensional aspect of your life force. This alignment adjusts your focus and consciousness into another dimensional flow. It moves you from one state of being into another experience of being. This brings a completely different perspective of you and your world. There is an instantaneous shift within you, a divine re-connection.

Some of the changes involve taking your place within the Collective Consciousness and moving yourself in a slightly new direction in order to see and understand more of a truth in the moment for you. The doors are wide open for you to take another powerful step within a new framework.

The timing of your activation of pre-agreements is perfect and you can just say yes to it. Simply feel the rightness of it through your heart and breathe. You have tremendous support within the Universe as you take this step.

The Pleiadians, Lemurians, and Spiritual realms continue to ask for a conscious connection to take place from you to them. They say it is a part of your awakening process to ask for specific assistance in your day-to-day lives.

As I stepped forward and consciously called forward support into my life, my whole world changed. It suddenly became much more open and flowing, as though every opportunity became alive. As I worked side-by-side with Spirit and the Pleiadians I felt as though I was working as part of a team. Gradually, as my trust grew with them, I was able to branch out more, giving detailed daily requirements of what I needed in my life, the support I needed to fulfill aspects of my mission projects, and support in being able to let go within my Self so I could move forward and not be bogged down by my third-dimensional human aspect.

I realized it was very important for me to create a structure for myself with my energetic team, so I created a time for daily morning meetings, like a board meeting, outlining the tasks at hand, asking for what I needed in fine detail. I asked for clarity, from the smallest to the largest things in my life. I realized that they did not know how this planet functioned third-dimensionally, so defining my needs helped them move with me to get the job done.

This structure supported me during my day. I would feel a closeness to my energetic alliances with each step I took. It was powerful and empowering to become part of a team. I also discovered how important it is for me to be a part of this working team. It accelerated a divine union that I was a part of, which activated a sacred webbing between me and the alliances within my team. It became a sacred experience. My heart expanded as I played out this new role, because I began to hold a new vibration of love through my heart and through these profound connections of love with my team. I found myself part of this divine union each morning.

I realize that my experience working closely to Spirit is important to share so that you can begin to understand how the interaction with them can support you. As you work closely with your energetic alliances they begin to understand you and your needs within your human aspect operating within this third-dimensional earth plane. This supports your pre-agreement alliances in a way that they can begin to understand how to support you within your mission as a human being.

Steps to Activate Energetic Pre-Agreements Through Conscious Choice

Audio file: Chapter 2
Audio file #2

1. Hold your heart with the palm of your hand, and bring your Conscious Awareness to your hand connecting to your heart.
2. Don't forget to use the Conscious Breath (in and out of the mouth), alternating with regular breaths every 30 seconds.
3. Come into the moment. Just Be with you, your hand on your body and your breath, nothing more.
4. Through your active Conscious Choice you call forth your pre-agreement to all energetic alliances now.
5. Let go. You might feel a strong energy move through you as you do this. It is because you are activating another level of your path in taking this step.

As you work with Audio File #2, let go and allow your experience. Open up to all that is here for you in the moment. Remember: As you hold your Self within the moment, you begin to align to many energetic aspects of your Self. Enjoy your unfolding experience!

After You Have Activated Your Pre-Agreement Energetic Alliances

It is through the telepathic center in the brain that you can align and fully utilize these new connections through your pre-agreements with the energetic realms. This activation process gives you an opportunity to open up and build your skills using your telepathic communication and communion. This will help you build an easy working relationship with the Spiritual realms and other energies with whom you have aligned. The Universe communicates through telepathic means. Now is your time to begin this activation.

Note: Read Chapter 3 and then download the audio files for your telepathic activation.

Pre-agreements With Others on This Earth Plane

You have made pre-agreements with other human beings on the planet, and these pre-agreements are important to activate now. You all come in with pre-agreements with certain groups of people and individuals. These groups or individuals that come into your lives to assist you are here to mirror certain things so you can grow into a self-loving process. Other people—your friends—are people who are here to support you, and within that friendship there are mutual missions that you have pre-agreed to accomplish with that person or with groups of people.

For some of you, now is the time to call forward your soul mate. Many of you will be re-connecting to your destiny person to learn and experience love in a very different way in order to heal internal wounds that have created a separation within you. Now you mutually let go and grow in love, fulfilling an important pre-agreement.

There are some soul groups that have pre-agreed to be together at this time to assist in anchoring grids, holding grid lines, and fulfilling projects together. Part of these soul group missions is to witness each other in the individual birthing process, as well as the birthing of a deep union within the full group. It is the time for us as human beings to turn back to each other and connect through a fourth/fifth-dimensional relationship, giving each other support by remembering together within sacred unions. We have to trust and love through a birthing of Truth, letting go of the separating thoughts of the ego, and working together in a state of union, consciously re-activating the divine connection within your group.

~~~

Beloved Ones,

We greet you. We open up to you a clear vision of your Selves at this moment. You are a central sun while everything else moves around you. You draw to yourself at this time all that you need, by Conscious Choice. This is the new energy that surrounds you. Part of this journey right now is a learning curve for you to understand your worth, to understand your power, and to understand the illusion of your world. It is a passage of moving from one reality of illusion, to the reality of Truth. This Truth is for you to receive your Self. For all that you are within your humanness and all that you are within your spiritual nature. We witness you in this transition of your Self. We witness your courage as you open into trust, not always understanding all that is taking place in the moment, but stepping forward with your heart and taking your place. Know that we hold you as you transition.

Love and blessings,
The Pleiadians

~~~

3

Activating Your Crystalline Structure

I have talked about the empowerment of Conscious Choice in your life, and right now you have a tremendous opportunity to awaken through your newly birthed crystalline structure. You are being given a gift and it is time for your awakening. Each one of you has an equal opportunity to move forward into this next transformation. It is not only the planet that is going through a dimensional shift from a third-dimensional planet to a fourth/fifth-dimensional planet; you are going through your own shift with an energetic birthing within your physical bodies. As the Earth goes through this multi-dimensional birthing process you are going through an electrical birthing process within your cells.

The energies within your body must align with the Earth in order for you to unite with and adjust to the energetic changes taking place on the planet. In addition to the physical changes happening within you, your consciousness is in a deeply transformative state. The whole planet is going through a powerful metamorphosis. This metamorphosis began very gradually at the beginning of 2009, when the Pleiadians spoke about the Self-Healing Prophesy energy being activated on the planet. This was a grace period that opened up for all human beings to receive support during your awakening in the New Dawning time.

The Pleiadians gave me this picture: Each time there is an earthquake or any sort of volcanic activity on the earth plane, a shaft of light is birthed, coming onto the earth plane. This creates a dimensional shift within the Earth's energy, anchoring a fourth/fifth-dimensional energy. At the same time, this light is also generating a multi-dimensional birthing of light within each cell of your body. These energetic changes were very subtle in the beginning, which was necessary because you needed to physically acclimate yourself to the changes. Each shift brought you into a different state of consciousness.

Imagine a dark room that has never seen light. Suddenly a window is opened light comes in for the very first time. This light has created a growing awareness within a small part of you, which expands each time light enters, creating transformation within you. This *birthing light* expanded the light frequency of each one of your cells, and every cell is responding to the awakening light that holds the unique divine essence of Self.

This small ray of light also began to birth across the earth plane, re-opening the energetic grid lines within the Earth and bringing the New Dawning energy to the Earth, trees, and rocks. There is a re-activation of the crop circles, which brings them to a new multi-dimensional level of activation. There is a network of alignments from the crop circles to all megalith sites on the planet, opening up energetic webbing across the planet, and a re-alignment of all the megalith sites, bringing them back to the original pure, sacred state of when they first anchored here on Earth. This network of alignments has created the birthing of a sacred webbing throughout the earth plane. This webbing creates a womb for the Principles for Living to be re-birthed through each one of you.

All the energies within the earth plane that have an energetic aura are being re-designed and re-aligned with this pure awakening light force within this sacred webbing structure.

On 11/11/11, there was a dynamic shift. Waves of a birthing light anchored onto the planet. The energies that came at that time brought a frequency of love that created new avenues for each one of you to move through. These doorways, which I liken to "a birthing channel of light," opened up to allow each person to link into individual aspects of their divine Self. Your cells were ready to hold and integrate higher levels of your light into your physical body. This allowed you to open and realign back into this new dimensional perspective of your relationship to your Spiritual Self.

A veil lifted on 11/11/11 for you to glimpse more of truth and who you are within your fourth/fifth-dimensional sacred heart. Simultaneously, you were moved out of the drama of the third-dimensional illusion, aligning you naturally back to your Spiritual Self. Many of you have stayed within this reconnection to Self. The memory anchored within your cells and you will never again be as fully engaged in third-dimension drama.

Each one of you has made a pre-agreement to receive this awakening. The pure light that birthed through you on 11/11/11 also birthed a crystalline structure through your body. Every human on the planet received this crystalline structure at that time. The structure birthed and anchored within the space between your cells. It was not activated. Now is the time through Conscious Choice to activate your own crystalline structure.

~~~

Let's talk about the qualities of the crystalline structure. This structure holds a pure frequency of light and acts like a transmitter, electrical in nature, and has an unlimited ability to hold the highest frequencies of your divine light. When fully activated, it will allow your full divine frequency of light to be held within your physical body. You choose the moment when you are ready for this aspect of your enlightenment process.

The crystalline structure within each of you holds a unique divine component, so no crystalline structure is the same. However, each individual crystalline structure contains a common element, the God consciousness, enabling all of you to have a direct experience of Oneness with each other. Know that this crystalline structure simply births you back and re-unites you with your natural spiritual state. This activation will change the energetic dynamic of your physical body, and it will allow you to hold the full energetic aspect of your divine light within the cells of your body. Up to this point, the greater aspect of your light has been held outside your body because your electrical system could not cope with this level of energy. Now that dynamic has changed with your crystalline activation.

Once you begin to activate your crystalline structure you will set in motion your own birthing process. It is time for you to move into a place of self-empowerment. This is what the New Dawning is about: You birthing you—anchoring the full energy of your enlightened Self within your physical body.

~~~

Why Have We Received This Crystalline Structure Now?

As these new fourth/fifth-dimensional openings birth, there are new levels of electrical energy slowly birthing within you. There are energetic grid structures re-emerging on the Earth, designed to assist in anchoring and aligning you to these fourth/fifth-dimensional energies. These grids support the expansion of a natural energetic electrical flow on the planet, and you are receiving this electrical flow through the cells of your body. You are a part of this new natural energetic flow. It's as though there is a subtle but powerful interconnection between you and all life force within the planet.

You are not separate; you are playing an integral part in this awakening process. You made pre-agreements to play out your individual part in this amazing transformational process as part of the Collective Consciousness. It is because of your crystalline structure that you can be a part of this powerful interconnection between you and all life force energies within your planet.

The Pleiadians' role is to give you access to a series of awakening codes that you can use through your Conscious Choice to activate your crystalline structure in the different crystalline sites within your body. You are going to need some assistance to adapt to the new electrical system that births through you as the crystalline structures begin to activate. The Pleiadians are here to assist you energetically so that you can fully integrate. The Lemurian energies are opening into an energetic alliance with the Pleiadians to assist you with these crystalline adjustments.

The Lemurians were present on Earth at the time of Atlantis, but the Atlantians were on the land and the Lemurians were under the sea. Both worked with the crystals. The Atlantians were scientific and the Lemurians were spiritual, working with the spiritual alignments of the crystals. Their role here is to support you in your physical transition as you birth your crystalline structure. The Lemurians specialize with crystalline structure and are able to assist you in the adjustment of your crystalline structure and the integration of your crystalline structure within your system. They can also assist you in assimilating your new electrical system within your body and energetic field as you move through this transformational process.

When activated, the crystalline structure rejuvenates the cells within your body through the electrical component that births through the cells. In turn, this brings your cells into a new state of energetic transformation. Your cells are capable of holding and integrating new and higher aspects of your divine light, what some would call your Higher Self.

When you begin to activate your crystalline structure, it is important to activate it in levels through the electrical layers. Within each layer there are many multi-dimensional levels of yourself to be birthed, opening up an unlimited amount of your potential. With these openings there is an acceleration of your enlightenment process.

Let's look at the different roles your crystalline structure can play within your body, depending on what area of your body holds the crystalline structure. Up to this point, the areas that house the crystalline structure are the brain, thyroid, heart, and spine. As you move deeper into this transformational time there will be new crystalline sites birthed within you.

Note: Some individuals will have different placements of crystalline structures sites within their bodies, depending on individual pre-agreements and their role within the New Dawning period. The following crystalline structures sites are, for most of you, where you need to have the activations.

The Brain

When activated, the crystalline structure within your brain re-activates your telepathic center. There are two parts to the telepathic center of the brain: one for telepathic communication and one for telepathic communion.

As you transmit your given sacred sounds into your crystalline structure, activation begins. Your crystalline structure recognizes your unique frequency within the sound, and there is a light that begins to birth/open within your crystalline structure. The light immediately begins to transmit an electrical light frequency pulse, which results in a re-opening of the telepathic center within your brain that, for most human beings, has not been used in this lifetime.

Opening the telepathic center within your brain gives you access to clear telepathic communication and communion with the spiritual realms. All communication within the Universe is through this telepathic system. So you begin to naturally re-align back into the Universal Consciousness network, back into your place within this spiritual arena, and back into the spiritual aspect of your home.

Telepathic communication will enable you to work within new energetic alliances to support you in your daily life here on Earth, because your ability to telepathically communicate will help you build spiritual relationships. It will bring you to a place within the energetic community within the Universal Consciousness. Through the use of your telepathic communication you will begin a natural realignment to these Principles for Living. This will shift your energetic placement within the collective energies of the Universe because, as you are awakened by these principles, you will be aligning with the rest of the Universe.

You will be able to link into and receive the help you need to navigate through these changing times and to complete mission projects. You cannot complete your projects alone. So your ability to telepathically communicate will open you up to the energetic community within the universe.

Opening up your ability to telepathically communicate with the spiritual realms will greatly assist you in activating and completing your pre-agreements. You have pre-agreements in place for support, specifically to receive information to understand your own process here on Earth, and how to fulfill your own destiny and your Divine Plan. This information and support will also help heal the separation within yourself by moving you back into a natural flow with the spiritual nature of your Self. Through the natural gift of telepathy you can receive a deeper understanding of truth that exists within the Universe.

An important part of your enlightenment process is to form a conscious re-union with all things in nature. There is tremendous wisdom and healing held within the powerful and sacred energies of your mother Earth and her elements. Your telepathic center enables you to commune with the natural forces, gaining another level of simple Truths that will bring you back to a centered place within yourself. It is time to come home, and part of your homecoming is communion with the elements of Earth.

The crystalline structure also activates the pineal gland, the thalamus, and the hypothalamus. Activation creates an opening in the sensory area of the brain, enabling your to receive, process, and retain information. It allows you to recognize truth and act on that truth in everyday situations.

For example, in the past you might have heard or recognized a truth that resonates with you for your life. You will say to yourself, "Oh, that is so important!," which is an "a-ha moment" for you. Yet, it is a common experience that within a day many people have forgotten that important truth. With this activation there will be a natural integration within you, and you will not be able to forget that truth. The a-ha moment will stay within your Conscious Awareness and it will continue to birth through you on multi-dimensional levels.

The Thyroid

The crystalline structure within the thyroid holds special qualities that open up to what the Pleiadians call your divine factor. Your thyroid is going through an enormous change of functioning. In reality, the thyroid is just presenting as having problems; the role of the thyroid is simply changing through the anchoring of your crystalline structure.

The thyroid's new role is to hold and transmit your divine factor. As you activate your crystalline structure there is a transmission of your divine element flowing outward from your crystalline structure. It moves into your heart space, blending the energy with your sacred heart elements. The divine factor that holds your unique frequency begins to flow outward into the Universal Consciousness, where you are received and recognized through the frequency of your sacred energy.

As your frequency goes outward into the Universe, your placement within the Universal Consciousness responds and opens up. This creates a forging of a re-alignment through you to your energetic place within the Universe. This is an anchored support system for your re-birthing process, re-opening doors for you to access home once more on a conscious level. The Living Principles activate an alignment process through you as your sacred frequency begins to open through your divine factor.

Note: The activation of your crystalline structure births an element of your divine energy. This divine aspect is pulsed through cells of your body and rejuvenates the cells. Every cell aligns to the energy of your divine essence for self-healing through all organs and cells. You are being designed to live a lot longer in this lifetime.

The Heart

As you consciously choose to activate the crystalline structure within your heart, electrical energy is birthed within the physical cells. This electrical energy opens up a new dimensional level within your heart, making it possible for an expanded aspect of your divine Self to birth through you. Your heart's ability to hold a higher frequency of light opens up a direct line to your divine intuition. Your heart will naturally begin to channel this light essence of Self, through your heart and out into the world. It helps you have a deeper heart connection with the spiritual energies with which you have made pre-agreements to work.

Your Sacred Heart can move into a more expanded role because it utilizes the new electrical impulses from within the crystalline space. Know that your crystalline structuring has an unlimited ability to hold expanded frequencies of your light and easily integrate the alignments of your sacred Self, anchoring them into the cells of your heart. Your heart begins a resurrection process with the activation of your crystalline structure. It holds a new fluidity within the electrical pulsing in your cells. This makes it possible for you to channel a higher frequency of love through your heart and into every cell of your body, activating a self-healing process.

So your heart takes on a new role as a "natural receiving station," similar to a satellite dish, which enables you to draw toward yourself all that you need. Your sacred heart is naturally where your heart's desire births and where you can manifest what you need for yourself in this lifetime.

It can also send your pulse of light outward, which carries your unique frequency out into the Universal Consciousness. As it goes out across the earth plane, it draws to you other soul connections that you are ready to experience.

Every cell begins to pulse what the Pleiadians call your "heartbeat of light." The Universal Consciousness, that Collective Consciousness, recognizes your unique signature and begins to send all that you need to fulfill your missions. This supports you in receiving your natural abundance that is part of your birthright, which is to be activated in this lifetime.

This electrical rewiring through your systems is birthing New Dawning energy through every cell. Picture a sun rising through every cell in the body and rays of light shooting through every cell, expanding the cells into multi-dimensional energy so you can house this beautiful aspect of yourselves through your cells.

The Spine

The most powerful of all the crystalline structures within your body has been anchored in the spine and housed within the spinal fluid. The spinal fluid has always held a sacred element within it, a divine content, containing a pure frequency of light. The makeup of the crystalline structure in the spine has a different quality and purpose than other areas of the body. It holds the highest levels of our sacred awakening energies and contains elements of your abilities for manifesting and self-healing.

The transmitting energies of this crystalline structure work within the nervous system and activate the memory process. This energy works within a fifth/sixth/seventh/eighth-dimensional alignment. The activation of this energy aligns you back to a sacred understanding of knowledge and truth.

The activation of the crystalline structure in the spine transforms the nervous system in order for you to cope with high electrical energy that you are going to be carrying with the activation of the crystalline structure in the other centers. This balances you and opens up the energy (what people call the kundalini energy), which is transforming with the crystalline structure. This crystalline structure operates directly through what is called the "God Head" and opens up a re-alignment to the highest order of your light. When you are ready, it re-unites you to sacred connections.

Once activated, these energies within the spine work in direct alignment with the heart's crystalline structure. *There is a series of dimensional-level activations required within the heart before the initial activation of your crystalline structure within the spine.* It is important to understand that you will not be successful with the activation of your crystalline structure within the spine until you have completed certain levels of dimensional activation within the crystalline structure in your heart.

The energies of the Earth play an important role, because once your crystalline structure is activated, the Earth's energies are going to be able to communicate with and through you, and you will have the ability to hold both the Earth and heaven elements within your physical form. This will assist you being a natural channel not only with spiritual realms, but with the sacred elements of nature. The crystalline structure in the spine holds a different quality because it allows you to channel through the pure aspects of the natural forces. The natural forces you need right now are going to assist you in a continuous unfolding and integration of this electrical energy, acting as an important balancer for you. As your electrical energy and the Earth's energy balance, you will automatically begin aligning with all the energetic grid lines opening on the earth plane. You will become a part of the natural flow of the Earth's energy through this transition time. The Pleiadians need many of you to be a natural conduit for some of these grid lines through the earth plane, especially as you birth these new dimensional energies within you.

Thyroid Crystalline Structure Activation

Audio File: Chapter 3
Audio file #1
Sacred sound: ANAE SHEAN

This position is called the Divine Access Point, or DAP. This is the area of the body in which the light of the Self can most readily enter the body. This is the soft area at the base of the throat just above the sternum. You are simply touching with the two fingers next to the thumb, no pressure. Your index finger and middle finger come together and touch this position. You can use either hand. Diagram A shows the correct position of the DAP for this activation.

✳ - Activation of crystalline structure in thyroid access point

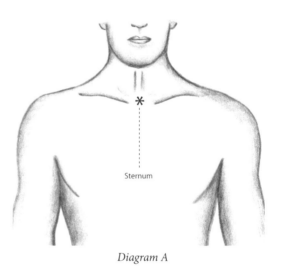

Sternum

Diagram A

Bringing your conscious awareness to this position opens a doorway. Move through the doorway and use the conscious breath, which will move you into the crystalline structure.

1. Begin by touching the DAP with the index finger and the middle finger very lightly. Bring your Conscious Awareness into the opening where your fingers are touching the DAP. Take a conscious breath. Let go.

2. As you bring your Conscious Awareness there, the doorway opens. You may see, sense, or feel the opening taking place. Bring your Conscious Awareness to where you are touching and take a conscious breath.

3. Allow yourself to enter the opening. Allow yourself to be moved in through the opening, into the crystalline structure within the thyroid. Take a conscious breath and let go.

4. Open up your Conscious Awareness into the space. Bring your Conscious Awareness to touch the crystalline structure within this space. Use your Conscious Breath into the crystalline structure. Allow your experience, letting go into the space of the crystalline structure.

5. Allow an opening, a deepening of the opening, within the crystalline structure within your thyroid. Now you begin to activate the alignment to your divine factor.

6. Allow your experience. Let your Conscious Awareness open up and touch where the energy is beginning to pulsate, form, or move around you. Bring your Conscious Breath into your crystalline form. Allow the birthing of this aspect, this divine aspect of yourself.

7. Allow the connection. You may see, sense, or feel energy pulsing from the crystalline structure into the cells of your body. Let go and allow yourself to open to the essence of your Self that is birthing through this interaction within the crystalline structure.

8. Bring the sacred sound ANAE SHEAN into the crystalline structure. Bring your unique frequency of the sound into your crystalline structure. Breathe and let go. Your crystalline energy is going to respond to your sound birthing another level of your divine factor. Let go into your experience.

9. Bring your sound right into the center of the crystalline energy, feeling your sound and becoming your sound. Feel, see, or sense how your crystalline structures are responding to the unique frequency of your sound.

10. Allow yourself to move into the opening within the crystalline structure as you continue to create the sacred sound ANAE SHEAN. Open up and allow another level of your sound to move into your crystalline structure. Breathe and let go.

11. Bring your full Conscious Awareness into the crystalline form that is birthing here from your sacred sound. Take a conscious breath and let go into the opening. Breathe and allow yourself to open into the light. Feel the essence of your divine factor within the crystalline structure flowing into the cells of your body.

12. Bring your Conscious Awareness deeper into the space. Use your Conscious Breath, like a soft breeze into your crystalline

structure, and move into another level of this dimensional opening within the structure itself. Breathe and let go. Take another soft breath into the space, feeling the essence of your light that is birthing from your divine factor within the crystalline structure. Allow your experience.

13. Then very slowly come back to where your fingers are touching the DAP at the base of the throat. You may feel that you are traveling back a long way through the multi-dimensional energies to your physical body. Take all the time you need to fully integrate this level of your divine factor, this essence of yourself through the cells of your body.

Just know that you will begin a new pathway as you activate your divine factor through this activation of your crystalline structure. Just let go and allow your Self to Be. Know that the Lemurian energies can support you in your activation process. Call them forward to be with you and give them permission to make adjustments within your system. Remember: They cannot come into your energetic space without your permission.

Heart Crystalline Structure Activation

Audio File: Chapter 3
Audio file #2
Sacred sound: KEE NAH AHH SAE

1. Begin by bringing the palms of your hands to your chest. Your heart area is the whole area of the chest between your shoulders. Bring your Conscious Awareness to your palms connecting to this area and take a Conscious Breath. Feel the warmth of your hands as you come fully into your heart space.

2. Bring your Conscious Awareness into your heart and open to get a sense of the crystalline structure within your heart space. Remember: The heart space can even be beyond the physical body, so your crystalline structure may feel really large. Don't necessarily look for it within the physical heart space; you may sense or feel it running through the heart space and expanding outward. Breathe and let go.

3. Bring your Conscious Awareness and take a Conscious Breath. By Conscious Choice you are opening up to connect to the energy or sense of your crystalline structure in your heart. Breathe and let go.

4. Allow your Conscious Awareness to touch your crystalline structure and take a breath. To expand, let go. Allow the energy to simply unfold. Allow the expression of the crystalline structure within the heart. Take a breath and bring your Conscious Awareness to touch another aspect of your crystalline structure.

5. Now you are ready to activate your crystalline structure in the heart. Use the sacred sound KEE NAH AHH SAE. Bring your unique frequency of sound into your heart center. Touch your crystalline structure with your Conscious Awareness and let go. Letting go allows you to go deeper into the crystalline form and into your heart. Let go and allow your experience.

6. Take a Conscious Breath and let go into the space. Let yourself follow the essence of the crystalline structure of your heart. Let yourself move through the space, touching where you feel with your Conscious Awareness. You may get a sense of the pulsing energy through the crystalline structure, like a "heartbeat of light" that starts to beat through the crystalline structure, sending these energetic pulses of your unique signature out into the Universe. Touch this energy with your Conscious Awareness.

7. Move your Conscious Awareness to the center of your crystalline structure. Touch it with your Conscious Awareness and bring the sacred sound KEE NAH AAH SAE into the central space. Bring at least three sounds into this central space.

8. Bring your Conscious Awareness into the opening created by your sound. Simply touch this opening and take a Conscious Breath. A veil lifts. When you feel ready, bring three more sacred sounds, KEE NAH AHH SAE, into the opening. Allow yourself to enter the opening of this space that takes you deeper into the crystalline structure of your heart.

9. Let your Conscious Awareness open into this dimensional webbing that is crystalline in structure. Allow yourself to become part of this webbing by using the Conscious Breath. Let go. Bring the sacred sound KEE NAH AAH SAE into the webbing to expand and align to this dimensional webbing. Allow your experience.

10. Bring the palms of your hands back to your chest. Bring your full Conscious Awareness to your heart. Feel yourself in the very center of this crystalline webbing within your full heart space. Let yourself open into the full element of this crystalline webbing. Do whatever you need to do in this moment with whatever is in front of you. Breathe and let go. Allow your full integration. Let go.

As you activate your crystalline structure within your heart, be aware that you may feel vulnerable as you birth and anchor a new aspect of your light within your heart. Don't forget to claim your heart and the beauty of your heart. Take time to hold your heart center physically during the day after the crystalline activation and use your Conscious Breath. This is a big step forward that you are consciously taking.

~~~

Beloved Ones,

There are many keys available for each one of you to utilize at this time for your awakening. It is about you finding your own unique key that is within your Self that will open a doorway that you can walk through.

Your individual keys can be found through your crystalline structure that is currently birthing through you. Each one of you has a unique aspect within your crystalline structuring. It allows you to move into a new awakened alignment with the spiritual realms and with all the family of light.

Know that you are part of the family of light, and today you are being asked to open up and consciously align to your place within "the family of light." This is your time to Be, to birth and celebrate all that you are. There never has been a time like the present for this resurrection process, "birthing you into Being."

All these keys can be revealed within your Self; your answers lie within. Don't be distracted by your third-dimensional illusion, move within your Self and be willing to ask: "What it is I am needing at this time to take my next steps?"

As you move into clarity of what your needs are, be willing to take your first step. This first step is to ask for support from us, the Pleiadians and the Spiritual realms. It's in the asking that the difficulty lies for many of you. It's as though you cannot believe that the support is possible, almost like you don't believe you deserve the help!

Part of your resurrection process is to reach out and ask for support. That is part of you taking back your power. This support is a part of your natural birthright. It is a part of your natural passage through to your self-awakening/ self-discovery. You see, you were never supposed to do this alone. You made pre-agreements to receive support at this most momentous time in your evolvement.

You are all being held in support of you taking your next step. There is so much love and appreciation for all that you are doing on the earth plane at this time.

Reach out—take your next step!

Blessings,
The Pleiadians

~~~

4

Activating Your Telepathic Communication and Telepathic Communion

You are now ready to begin the activation of your crystalline structure within your brain. I want to remind you of the significant step you are about to take.

The crystalline structure within the brain also re-activates the pineal gland, the thalamus, and the hypothalamus. This activation creates an opening in the sensory area of the brain enabling you to receive, process, and retain information. It allows you to recognize truth and to act on that truth in everyday situations. This next step reconnects you to an ability to work with your telepathic communication and telepathic communion. It brings you back into a place of self-empowerment on your path, to move toward completing your pre-agreement energies, because you will be able to communicate more directly with your energetic alliances and with all life force energies within the Universal Consciousness. This step brings you back to your place and to playing your role within the Collective Consciousness. You fulfill an aspect of your mission with this activation.

The awakening of your telepathic center not only activates a remembering for you, but you also begin to glimpse aspects of your natural gifts. It allows you to accept your place within the Universal Consciousness because you can communicate and participate within the Universe. It will allow you to work through the network with all life force within the Universe. Your newfound abilities will link you in to experience an aspect of your magical Self that functions naturally within the fourth/fifth-dimension realms.

I want to share an experience I had that might support you in your next step. A short time ago, I experienced my first connection with the Lemurians. Up until then my main body of work was with the Pleiadians, Mother Mary, Jesus, and Sai Baba. I had a profound and powerful awakening that opened up my Lemurian aspect of Self. A crystalline structure birthed through all the cells of my body. This opened up an awareness of the sacred path that the Lemurians are holding for all of us human beings at this time. It showed me an aspect of the "Grand Plan" and the Lemurians' role with us as we sit on the threshold of our awakening through the activation of our own individual crystalline structures. I was awed by the profound dimensional space from which they emerged and the soft energy of love as they enfolded me during my deep birthing process. I was re-united with my pre-agreement to work with the Lemurians. At that time, a new golden pathway opened up before me. This pathway showed me my new direction and linked me into a crystalline dimensional flow that I now know allowed a transformation and transmutation to take place. This crystalline link took me back to profound understandings and clarity of my purpose that made it possible for me to move into a place of being, ending aspects of separation within my human aspect. I was also connected to an understanding and truth of reunion and realignment with home, which is beyond words for me.

The Lemurians are here at this time to assist all of you who are willing to open up and call them forward. Both the Pleiadians and Lemurians held open a platform of energy so that I could see the completed plan for each one of us here on the earth plane, and they shared with me the part that I was to play at this time within this grand plan.

An energetic alliance is now being activated between the Pleiadians and the Lemurians. The synergy of the alliance is pure light and is very powerful. This alliance enables each one of us to be moved through an assisted birthing process within our crystalline structure in the telepathic center of our brains. This support is essential for you to fully achieve this activation because of the many multi-dimensional levels to be activated. They will help you integrate and adjust to the new electrical components through your body from these activations. This grand plan was never meant for you to accomplish it alone.

Even though you have a pre-agreement in place with the Lemurian energies, this agreement can only be activated with your conscious permission. You have free will as a human being, which is always honored. Your pre-agreement will activate very simply by connecting through your heart, calling forth the Lemurians, and acknowledging the pre-agreement that was made between you.

The Activation of Your Telepathic Center

The activation of your telepathic center will enable you to begin a unique communication with all life force groups within the Universe. Part of your mission is to establish a working relationship with these different groups and participate fully in your role at this New Dawning time. Human beings are one of the many life force groups within the Universe, and the only group still operating from the third-dimensional state.

There are a series of alien groups to which the Pleiadians and the Serians belong. Within the spiritual realms there are many groups: the Angels, the Light beings, the Masters, the Natural Forces within the earth plane that operate outside third dimension, the mineral kingdom, the plant kingdom, and the animal kingdom. These are just some of the life force groups that make up the Universal Consciousness. All life force within the Universe are part of a certain life force group.

You will be able to communicate with these groups through the sacred reconnections from the activation of your telepathic center. Your birthing process will begin as a collective effort between you activating your own crystalline structure within your telepathic center, the Pleiadians giving you the sacred tools, and the Lemurians assisting by adjusting your crystalline structure.

At this New Dawning time you are moving back to a place of your personal power. You get to choose the time to activate the crystalline structure. Let's talk about how the crystalline structure re-aligns you to your natural ability for telepathic communication and how it moves you to remember this ability.

Each time you consciously choose to open into your telepathic center there is an accelerated opening within your crystalline structure, which makes it possible for another level of your light to birth through the cells of your body. This brings you into another dimensional aspect so you gradually re-align back to your divine experience.

There are two telepathic centers in the brain:

1. **Telepathic Communication:** If you want to send a message, it will be received in the full form without any misunderstanding.
2. **Telepathic Communion:** This opens the door to a loving frequency of Oneness as you align, perfectly sharing a moment with a common purpose. It is the exchanging of an experience in its purest form.

All life force groups within the Universe communicate through telepathic communication, with the exception of human beings on Earth. As stated earlier, humans are the only life force group still operating within the third-dimensional illusion. The third-dimensional space involves the full ego mind, and telepathic communion cannot operate through the ego. Many of you are moving beyond the third-dimensional illusion and spending time within the fourth/fifth-dimensional realms, and then coming back into a third-dimensional human experience when you need to be there.

It is important to bypass the ego mind by opening into your fourth/fifth-dimensional Self in order to work with your telepathic communication. You can do this simply by bringing you, Conscious Awareness down to your heart center. Use your Conscious Breath. As you do this your energy moves away from the ego mind to your heart. Remember that your connection to Self is through your heart. Be aware that you do not have to bypass the ego mind all of the time. You simply need to work through your heart center as you work with your telepathic communication center.

Know that telepathic communication is a natural part of you, and activating your telepathic communication center is returning you to one of your natural states. The more you utilize your telepathic communication center, the more anchored and expanded you will be within this state.

Telepathic communication uses thought transference. Thought transference is placing a completed concept of informational details from the telepathic center of one being to the telepathic center of another being. This ability allows for clarity in communication so complete and pure that there is absolutely no possibility of confusion within your communication. Many of you who channel information have the experience of receiving your information through this format.

This telepathic imprint comes in a multi-dimensional form with many aspects of energies woven into the transmission, which may contain love, appreciation, and support. This telepathic transmission can be likened to being multi-colored and multi-dimensional in form, with perfect precision.

The Pleiadians are going to give you a series of steps to take so you will be able to begin activating your crystalline structure. They have a set of tools to give you for this re-activation:

Sacred Sound

The sacred sound is something you are going to speak. You will bring forth the sound into the crystalline structure. Each one of you holds a unique signature within this sacred sound. Your crystalline structure recognizes this unique signature and responds to your frequency within the sacred sound, creating an activation of brilliance within your crystalline structure.

Thought Code

You actually place the thought code in the crystalline structure with your consciousness and it holds a higher frequency of vibration than the actual sound. It is a telepathic thought code that you will place, not speak, and this opens up your telepathic communion. It activates a high frequency of the God essence, of pure loving force that allows you to commune with the Collective Consciousness God energy.

Hand Muhdrah

This is a physical hand position. As you bring your Conscious Awareness into the hand position it activates a dimensional pathway to align you within your telepathic center.

Code Forms

These Code Forms are pure in nature and designed by the Pleiadians to support you in re-birthing and expanding your telepathic center, as well as activating other levels of your crystalline structure in your telepathic center in order to accelerate your abilities for expanded communication.

Code Forms are designed to support your entire system within your cells to create an integration of the new electrical energy birthing through your system as you use your telepathic center. They also activate elements of your own divine aspect to anchor through the cells of your body, accelerating your awakening process.

You will be given a series of Code Forms to work with, beginning on a base level with Code Form #1 and working through to Code Form #6. You will be able to slowly build and expand your telepathic center by moving into the more complex, higher energy Code Forms. Look at Diagram B on page 53, which shows the six Code Forms, and follow the guidelines to work specifically with each Code Form individually.

Telepathic Communication

The crystalline energy activated in your second telepathic center anchors a communion energy and a communion of oneness not only of thought, but of essence; a blending between one energetic alliance and another. The telepathic communion center holds the sacred alignment of the essence of all life force. If I brought my communion energy to you, you would experience my essence and a Oneness of total connection. The communion energy can also pass on knowledge, clarity, and Truth.

Six Code Forms

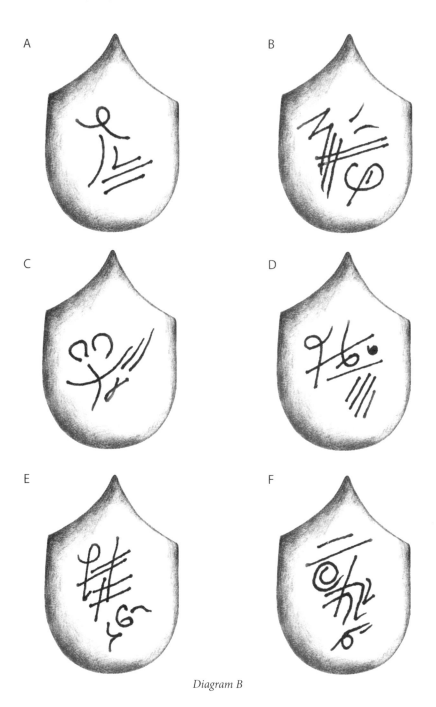

A

B

C

D

E

F

Diagram B

Telepathic communion carries a much higher frequency of dimensional light than telepathic communication. It transmits not only an understanding, but an innate total connection. It is not just a message; it is a blessed union, a Oneness, which is why it is called communion. All life force groups within the Universe work from this space.

Your crystalline structure holds your unique divine aspect as well as the element of the God Consciousness. So the activation of this crystalline center brings you into full alignment with all life forces within the Universe, making sacred communion possible.

It is important to understand that, at this time, most human beings are limited in their ability to have a full telepathic communion experience. You have a tendency to keep separate from each other in many ways because you don't trust each other with your hearts. You had reasons to stay separate as a human being, with many experiences throughout lifetimes that have taught you that it is not safe to open up fully with our hearts. This is part of the human experience on the third-dimensional plane. It will take some time before many of you will be ready to move beyond this separated state. The activation of your crystalline structure is going to help you forge this pathway back to each other so you can live in the New Dawning era in a very different state of consciousness.

You may already know a few human beings with whom you can be more vulnerable. You may find that you will be able to telepathically align with people you have made pre-agreements with, but because of the human ego you are not always going to telepathically engage. Ideally, there will come a time when that doorway will open and you will be able to find a stable sacred union with each other.

Audio File #3 will assist you to journey telepathically with a chosen life force group within the Universe. Choose one of your pre-agreement alliances to work with or an essence that you have previously worked with on other levels so you are comfortable opening into a sacred telepathic communion.

The Pleiadians and the Lemurians are asking us to work primarily with a telepathic communion experience. This means you need to let go and open into a sacred communion. This means choosing an alliance energy you are able to trust. You always have a choice whether to open to the sacred communion or just telepathic communication, which does not include the experience of Oneness. Remember: This is a beginning, and each step you take is important for you. You select what you are ready to do now, knowing that you honor your Self with each step you take.

Great things can be achieved through a group consciousness. When I refer to "group consciousness" I include all life force groups throughout the Universe. You are a part of this grand plan, and you can contribute your sacred essence to the Collective Consciousness. The Universe will benefit from your participation fulfilling your mission at this important time on the planet.

Each one of you has a lot of work to do. It is a powerful and glorious work, not only for your individual Self, but for the planet. Every moment you awaken impacts every human being on the planet because of your God connection. This interconnection with each other is all a part of you.

Exercise #1: Activating Your Telepathic Center

Audio file: Chapter 4
Audio #1
Thought code: EE NAE
Sacred sound: ANAE SHEAN

Note: Your Conscious Breath is in and out of the mouth, breathing in deeply through the mouth and letting the breath go out through the mouth, without holding on.

Do this about once a minute.

Remember: Each time you choose to let go, you move into another level of re-alignment.

1. Touch your third eye position with your index finger. Note: You will physically be in the third eye position, but you will be entering a different dimensional opening from your third eye.

2. Bring your Conscious Awareness to the index finger on your third eye; feel the opening of the doorway and feel your Self being drawn into the opening. Use your Conscious Breath and let go into the opening. It might feel like a spiral energy taking you in. It may feel like you are going into a tunnel. Just allow your experience—breathe and let go. Each time you take a Conscious Breath and let go, you move deeper into this dimensional doorway.

3. Feel yourself come to the end. You are no longer expanding through the space, but instead where the crystalline structure is in your brain center. Just reach out and touch the space with your Conscious Awareness. Breathe into it and feel how the energy responds to the touch of your consciousness. Allow your experience. Note: You may see, feel, or sense this crystalline structure. Your experience may be subtle or strong. This does not matter, and does not impact your ability to activate your crystalline structure.

4. Bring your thought code EE NAH into the crystalline structure. It's as though you place it with your consciousness within the structure. Feel how the structure begins to respond to the

thought code. The structure may begin to light up, become fluid, and expand. You may begin to feel an expansion of energy, of heat, peace, joy. Allow your experience and let go. Use your Conscious Breath and breathe into the crystalline structure.

5. You will place your thought code EE NAH two more times. Send the second thought code and wait for a full expression and integration from the crystalline structure before sending the third thought code, EE NAH.

You will now begin using your sacred sound into the full structure. Remember: The crystalline structure will recognize your unique divine signature within your frequency of sound, moving the structure into another level of birth.

Sacred sound: ANAE SHEAN

Use the sacred sound as many times as you feel to do so. Know that each sacred sound will expand or transform your crystalline structure.

Note: Activation begins as you transmit your sacred sounds into your crystalline structure. Your crystalline structure recognizes your unique frequency, and there is a light that begins to birth/open within your crystalline structure. The light immediately begins to transmit an electrical light frequency pulse, which results in a re-opening of the telepathic center within your brain that, for most human beings, has not been used in this lifetime.

Exercise #2: Aligning Your Hand Position to Your Telepathic Center

Audio file: Chapter 4
Audio #2

1. You will bring yourself into your telepathic center as you did in Audio #1.
2. Hold your right hand upright with all fingers closed, including the thumb, with your palm facing away from you. Note: See the hand position in Diagram C for reference.
3. Bring your full Conscious Awareness from your telepathic center to your hand. Feel the opening of the energy, like a doorway. Breathe into the doorway and let go.
4. As the doorway of the hand position expands in some way, begin to bring your

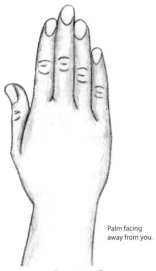

Palm facing away from you.

Diagram C

Conscious Awareness from your hand, slowly moving back into your telepathic center. Feel how a pathway begins to link your telepathic center and your hand position. It may feel like a line, bridge, pathway, or just an energetic link. Keep breathing and letting go; allow this connection to expand and express itself.

5. Bring your Conscious Awareness into the hand and feel the opening of the doorway within your hand position. Enter the doorway with your Conscious Awareness and follow the pathway/line/bridge link into your telepathic center. Open your full Conscious Awareness into the energy of your telepathic center, allowing your Self to fully open into the energy with your Conscious Breath. Note: Now you are able to enter your telepathic center through the opening of your right hand. This will make it much easier for you to link quickly within your telepathic center.

Initiating With Your Code Forms for Energetic Alliances

Audio file: Chapter 4
Audio #3

1. Bring your right hand upward into its position.
2. Bring your Conscious Awareness into the hand and feel the opening of the doorway within your hand position. Enter the doorway with your Conscious Awareness and follow the pathway/line/ bridge link into your telepathic center. Let your Self open your full Conscious Awareness into the energy of your telepathic center, allowing your Self to open into with your Conscious Breath.
3. Open to the Code Form A with your full Conscious Awareness. You will begin to feel it slowly being absorbed by your telepathic center. This turns your bridge to ON. Note: ON means there is an activation within your crystalline structure. Let go and allow your birth to take place. The energy of this Code Form is expanding your telepathic center and birthing another level of your crystalline structure within the cells of your body. Allow your full birth by breathing and letting go; allow your re-alignment to take place. You have six Code Forms to initiate into, and each Code Form is multi-dimensional in nature. This means there is an unlimited amount of initiation to receive from each phase of each Code

Form. Refer back to Diagram B on page 53 for your six Code Forms. **NOTE: Do no more than one Code Form activation per week.**

4. Activate your telepathic pathway by bringing your consciousness into your hand position. You will access your telepathic center.

5. Expand out your telepathic connection by bringing your consciousness into your hand position and letting go. It is through letting go that a deeper alignment can take place within your telepathic center.

6. Find Code Form A shown in Diagram D. Place your Conscious Awareness into the Code Form A within the box. Open to the Code Form A with your Conscious Awareness. Feel it absorbing through your telepathic center. This turns your bridge to ON.

7. Place the Code Form A from your telepathic center toward your desired connection. As the Code Form A is received by the desired connection, the telepathic lines are opened.

Diagram D

8. Feel the lines of energy open between you and the desired energy. Feel your Self being received. Open to this telepathic communion or communication.

9. This is your telepathic center. When this telepathic connection is complete, you get to turn it OFF by bringing your right hand down.

There are three audio files, 15 minutes in length, that assist you in activating these centers and enable you to work within your telepathic center. You learn to re-activate and expand your ability to work with your telepathic communication and your telepathic communion skills.

Activating your telepathic center is a big step forward for you. Remember the support systems that are in place for you through the Pleiadians and Lemurian energies, and your own pre-agreement alliances. Know that my energy is here to support you in this powerful awakening process.

~~~

A Special Message From the Pleiadians

It is through the telepathic center in the brain that you will align and utilize these connections with these portals of light. A series of electrical pulsing pathways are birthing within your crystalline structure, creating a new opening within your physical body. Today you will be opening up into these new states within you. They are like portals within your physical frame that are waiting to birth.

Blessings,
The Pleiadians

~~~

Beloved Ones,

It is the time to take another step on your path. This involves being willing to take your place in a new way within your world. It is the time to be willing to expand out your consciousness; to hold all human beings within a flowing fluid place of interconnection within you through your God consciousness. It does not mean you need to embrace the lower energies of the ego of each human being, but to open to the God consciousness that exists within each human on this earth plane no matter how buried it appears to be.

As you do this there is a sacred web that begins to birth through the planet, and this Sacred web begins to spin, assisting in the awakening of Truth on your planet. This is love in action birthing through you. Through that love births this sacred connection that you activate with your conscious choice.

The God essence "Oneness" does exist and you can make the difference by activating this connection consciously and holding the truth of this connection within your heart. It is time for your next step and it will expand your own capacity to BE.

We hold you as you take this next step forward.

Blessings,
The Pleiadians

~~~

5

Harnessing the Energy of the Earth's Natural Forces: Sacred Communion With Nature

The Pleiadians are responsible for transmitting all the sacred shamanic rituals, teachings, and knowledge to all native people on the earth plane many lifetimes ago. I want to share a piece about my initiation into the shamanic worlds that happened many years ago.

About 12 months before I came to this country, a Native American woman gave me a sacred pipe. I didn't realize the significance of receiving one, so I took the pipe thinking I could hang it on the wall in my house. When I sold all of my things before leaving Australia nobody wanted the pipe. Finally, my girlfriend said she would take it.

When she came to visit me about eight months later, she asked if I had received the pipe in the mail. I told her no, and she seemed concerned, but I reassured her that I didn't want it anyway.

Three weeks later the pipe arrived in the mail. When I unwrapped the package and held the pipe, I was immediately transported into a sacred lodge. Before me were the elders of the sacred lodge. This setting held a very different energy than I had ever experienced before. I likened it to a wild ocean storm. As I moved into this experience, there was a great power pouring through me. I was being asked to take a pledge of the pipe into my heart.

The feeling of responsibility around this experience was so overwhelming that I just threw the pipe down and said, "No, I'm not doing this. I don't know what this means. I don't understand what I am being asked to do!"

I was scared within these new energies. They were totally unfamiliar to any experience I had previously. The next morning I woke up about 5 o'clock and knew that the next step was to take the pipe into my heart. So I took the pipe to the sweat lodge that was in the direct line of powerful Mount Shasta. I took the pledge of the pipe into my heart. In that moment I was filled with a tremendous power and a language started coming through me. I didn't understand the language, but the energy was so strong it completely overwhelmed me. I was never the same after that.

I didn't use or even pick up the pipe very much after that, but the language would come through me every time I touched the pipe. And even when I didn't touch the pipe it would, at times, come through. On my birthday in January I was told I should do a ceremony with the pipe. I went outside and sat with the pipe; it was then that I was shown the power coming through me was my own Divine Energy.

This was a significant turning point in my life. I started to embody my power and receive it into my cells. Up to that time I'd been working and feeling and experiencing energy, but I had never realized that it was me. So I started to consciously open up to allowing it to live in the cells of my body. This process of consciously receiving my power created an acceleration of my awakening process. Through this powerful realization I began to consciously receive my full identity, which moved me into an alignment of my full mission. This all happened in 1992.

In this New Dawning time all human beings have been given the grace to receive the full alignments from the natural forces. With the crystalline structure activated you can come back through a sacred cycle to re-enter the "light wheel" of your awakening and end your separation. You can, through Conscious Choice, open to this natural union.

An important piece of your enlightenment process is to form a conscious reunion with all parts of nature. There is tremendous wisdom and healing held within the powerful and sacred energies of our Mother Earth and her elements. Your telepathic center enables you to commune with the natural forces, gaining another level of simple truths that will bring you back to a centered place within yourself. It is time to come home, and part of your homecoming is communion with the natural forces on the earth plane.

Your enlightenment process actually depends on you forming an energetic alliance with the natural forces. Finding this path will open you on another level to a sacred component within you. I liken this to finding a key to a door. There is a sacred doorway that will bring you into unique beauty and joy that has seldom been experienced. This doorway gives you access into the natural forces and opens up a powerful aspect of your Self, to what the Pleiadians call the internal Warrior.

The Warrior aspect of you is alive, powerful, and aligned to the pure and true life energy found within the natural forces. You have your own place within the natural forces, and your Warrior Self is waiting for you here. This Warrior part of you is essential for your next steps, because it opens you to multi-dimensional sacred aspects within you.

For lifetimes there has been a certain level of access to the natural forces on the earth plane with only a limited relationship with the trees, rocks, mountains, oceans, rivers, flowers, animal kingdom, insect world, and the elements of the sun, wind, fire, and Earth. The natural forces have always been here to provide nourishment for you to draw upon and to support you in your physical healing. Now it is time to allow the natural forces to teach you and to act as a mirror, so you can awaken to your own God essence that is alive within all nature and within yourself.

As this New Dawning shifting of consciousness has begun, a new opening has birthed and continues to birth between human beings and the natural forces. It began in 2009 and continues to accelerate through 2013 and beyond. The Earth is going through a dimensional birthing and so are the cells of your body, rejuvenating you. A grace period has opened, which gives everyone complete access to this connection with the natural forces on the earth plane.

As you move into alignment with the natural forces, you will be nutritionally fed from the Earth's energy—from the wind, from the water, from the spirit of the fire, and from the energy of the rising sun. As you journey back within each natural element and align through your telepathic center, you will receive an energetic nutrition flowing from each natural element into the cells of your body. This nutrition rejuvenates and births a multi-dimensional energy within you, bringing you into a direct alignment with aspects of your Warrior Self.

Know that now is the time for you to activate your Warrior energy. You will need this component within you during the New Dawning period. The Pleiadians speak of your transformational path that returns you to the magical age of renewal. This is the time you have all been waiting for, to leave the old behind and step forward into different realms where you truly belong.

The Earth will continue to transform, and it is important that you take your next step knowing that this will support the energy of the Earth. You can hold energetic grids steady on the Earth through your Warrior energy. You might find that many of you will gather and connect with an advanced telepathic communion once you have activated your Warrior energy.

The Pleiadians talk about aspects of your Warrior Self: A Warrior is someone who has taken courage to do battle with the inner enemies in order to face the truth of themselves and their world.

The four attributes of the Warrior are:

1. Harmony of spirit.
2. Honor of Mother Earth and the natural forces.
3. Humility toward your emotions.
4. Humor toward all the "stuff" of the ego mind.

The way of the Spiritual Warrior is a path of transformation—not easy, not quick—but real.

To become a Warrior means to be in your center. It is:

- In your essence (innocence), you live with trust and faith in the ultimate rightness and justice of the Universe, even though what is happening might try to knock you off center in every possible way.
- To not be affected by anyone or anything, anywhere, anytime, in any way.
- "Walking your Talk" as a Warrior of the Spirit, touching the world with beauty wherever you go in the Great Vision Quest Called Life. It is about finding your true purpose in becoming incarnate at this time, and gaining access to the inner strength and the tools necessary to materialize your chosen dreams through the great teachings of Mother Nature.

The Pleiadians describe this time of aligning back to your Warrior Self as "heaven on Earth," because you have the opportunity to begin a new path within your Self, create a new relationship within your Self as you begin to work with the natural forces, and as you begin to awaken this new aspect of your Self.

As you receive your Self it is like a sun rising over the horizon, and as each aspect of your sun's rays enter the cells of your body, you can transform. Your awakening happens as you begin to meet the energy of the natural forces, with the understanding that within this energy you meet your Warrior Self.

It is important to begin simply. You will find that your Warrior nature will quickly re-birth itself on many levels. You can start a level of this rejuvenation process as you work with the natural forces, working with a telepathic communion to connect with the Earth. This step will begin to align you into a different state of consciousness. You will begin to move into an energetic spiritual flow with the natural forces, and your telepathic communion abilities will transform by holding and expanding within this sacred flow.

This flow aligns you to aspects of your Warrior Self, which will enable you to live much longer than you could imagine possible. You will actually start reversing in age, and you will move into living 150 years to 200 years as you re-align to your Warrior Self. You will begin to experience a lot more of life in a fuller way than ever before. As you work within the natural forces and open into your Warrior self, a new area of your brain opens up and you enter into a profound state of self-healing.

You will begin to connect into the natural alliances within nature. As you create these sacred telepathic communion alliances you will begin to blend into a natural healing spring of flowing life force energy. This is the spiritual energy held within all nature. As you open into your place, you begin to have access to this energy for your Self.

Remember: The natural forces are part of these life force groups that the Pleiadians have previously talked about. As you move toward the natural forces, it is possible for you to go into a different level and state of union with those life force groups. As you go into this state of union you will discover a new level of your life force energy with which you can re-connect.

You can work with any one component of nature that appeals to you and draws you in. It does not matter whether it is one flower, one drop of dew on a leaf, a mountain, a tree, a bird, the sun, or an ocean. It does not matter because all life force exist within all nature. The connection just simply *is*.

The energies of the natural forces are going to reveal themselves to you in a whole new way as you open up your conscious telepathic communion toward them. There's going to be a communication with all levels of the natural forces: the animal kingdom, the plant world, and the mineral kingdom.

The veils have lifted and the Earth is birthing in consciousness. So are you.

Natural Forces

Let's talk about how you can specifically work with the natural forces to begin your sacred alignments back to your Warrior Self:

Working With the Sun

1. The time to work with the sun is just before sunrise. Bring your right hand up to align to your telepathic center, and open up your telepathic communion energy toward the sun's consciousness. Let go into the telepathic communion and allow yourself to breathe. Just Be. Allow your birth!

2. The moment that the sun breaks over the horizon, the sun shoots a nutritional substance through its telepathic connection with you. This new connection goes into the cells of the body for

regeneration. If you let yourself work with this piece, you will be amazed at how quickly you align, and are fed and rejuvenated through the sun.

Working With the Wind

When you feel the wind on your face, hair, or any area of your body, bring your consciousness to feel the element of the air. Open up your telepathic center with your right hand position and work with the essence of the wind. The energies are different than those of the sun, Earth, and fire. There is an element or essence of light present with the wind. Shut your eyes and allow your telepathic center to receive this pure essence. You will not be able to perceive the full essence of the wind without your telepathic communion center open. Just let go and allow your full experience. Allow yourself to be taken, adjusted, and moved within your Self. When this feels complete, close off by moving your right hand down.

Working With the Fire

To work with the fire you need to connect to the spirit of the fire.

1. Open up your telepathic center through your right hand position, and expand into your telepathic communion center.
2. Bring your consciousness into an area of the fire that calls you.
3. The essence of the spirit of the fire is compelling, drawing forth an aspect of your Warrior energy within you. Allow the full expression of your Warrior energy as it begins to come forward. Let go and open into your experience.
4. To disconnect from the telepathic connection with the fire, bring your full consciousness to your hand position and then close off your hand position by bringing your hand down.

Working With the Earth

Your Earth Mother's energy is here to support you in your transition. One of the most significant tasks for each one of you on the earth plane is to let go of all that you are holding onto from your third-dimensional illusion experiences. Part of the Earth's role is to take from you the burdens of your struggle, guilt, shame, fear, sadness, and all the pieces you are holding on to and carrying with you.

All you need to do is to lie or sit on the Earth. Bring your consciousness into this physical connection you have with the Earth and simply breathe. Let go of all that you are holding on to from your past.

Your Earth Mother asks you to let go so you can move into a series of sacred re-alignments back to Self. The Earth is also playing a major role in supporting each one of you, assisting you to integrate the new electrical energy that is birthing through your cells at this time.

It helps to take off your shoes and socks and allow the bottom of your feet to be on the earth, and at the same time have the palms of your hands resting on the earth. This allows a circular energy from the earth to move through all the systems within your body. Use your Conscious Breath and just let go into the earth, allowing the integration and re-alignments to occur.

Working Telepathically With the Earth

1. Lie or sit on the earth and feel your physical connection to the earth. Open up your telepathic connection through your right hand position. Take your time to expand your Conscious Awareness into the hand position, fully expanding the opening.
2. Then follow the opening into your telepathic center. Let go and allow the full expansion.
3. Bring your consciousness toward your physical connection to the earth. Allow the full expression of your telepathic communion with the earth. It's important to let go and allow your full multi-dimensional experience.
4. When complete, come back to your right hand and consciously disconnect by bringing your hand down.

Sacred Communion With Nature

Communing with nature involves working with any one element that is a part of the natural forces. Choose any element that calls to you. It could be a tree, mountain, or rock—whatever draws you.

1st process: Choose the natural element that you wish to telepathically link

1. Bring your right hand upward and link through your hand position, opening up to your telepathic center. Open up to your Code

Form A; feel it absorb into your telepathic center. (Code Form A is shown in Diagram D.)

2. Bring your Code Form A toward your desired element, feel the element receive your Code Form, and feel the telepathic alignment begin to open.
3. Open up into a full telepathic communion.
4. When complete, consciously disconnect by bringing your right hand down.

Diagram D

2nd process: This telepathic process involves using a rattle

1. You begin by tapping your heart center three times with your rattle and then creating a pathway with your rattle from your heart to the element with which you have chosen to telepathically connect. You use your rattle to create a pathway, rattling to the element, connecting to the element, and then rattling back along the pathway to your heart. You are actually building a dimensional pathway between you and your chosen element. You continue to work with this process until the pathway feels complete. Note: Understand that your rattle creates a further dimensional opening for you to enter, enabling you to connect into a fuller telepathic communion with your element.
2. Open up your hand position to create your telepathic opening and bring your rattle to the element. It may feel as though you are meeting a different dimensional expression of your natural element.
3. When this feels complete, bring down your right hand and consciously disconnect the telepathic connection.

The Journey to Make Your Medicine Circle

Making your own medicine circle is a central aspect of your journey back to your Self as the Warrior. Know that you will never be the same once you choose to take this step. You will enter your sacred circle one way and leave your sacred circle changed.

What You Need

To set up your medicine circle you need:

- Rattle or drum.
- Water.
- Compass.
- Tobacco.
- Sage and matches.

When setting up your medicine circle, always place a small amount of tobacco on the ground with a prayer of thanks to Great Spirit. This is positioned where you are about to place your central stone and it is also done for each one of your four directional stones.

1. Place your central stone in your circle. This will be your alignment to Great Spirit, the Earth Mother, Father Sun, Mother Moon, Grandmothers, Grandfathers, and to your Ancestors. It also anchors you to the above and below worlds.

2. Place your first stone beginning in the South, West, North, and finally in the East. You will need a compass to locate these positions accurately. Your East direction is your doorway. Place two large stones to act as a door "frame" with a smaller stone between to act as a door (enter and exit your circle). This smaller stone is your East direction. Note: Look at Diagram E to see how your East door is constructed.

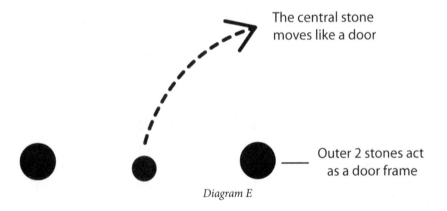

The central stone moves like a door

Outer 2 stones act as a door frame

Diagram E

3. Once you have your four stones in place, fill in your circle with smaller stones. Begin in the East direction and move clockwise around toward the South, West, North, and finish in the East. Instead of stones you can use some cornmeal, sprinkling it from the East stone clockwise, filling in your circle.

4. When your circle is completely filled in, bring your belongings into your circle and then light your sage to smudge your circle. Note: Your doorway, the central stone (in the East), must be closed before you begin the smudging process. Smudging your circle opens up the energy in your circle, creating a clear space in readiness for you to do your own sacred work, opening up the space for you to connect to the elements within your four directions. The smudging opens up the energy of the circle to act as a womb, holding you as you birth.

Note: You begin the smudging process at the central stone. From the central place of your circle, move with your lit sage around the central place of your circle in a slow movement, gradually moving outward in a spiral-like movement through your whole circle to the outer edge. You can enter/exit your circle only through the doorway in the East.

To Activate Your Circle (Claiming Your Self Within Your Sacred Circle)

Now you are ready to activate your circle. Let your Self go as you activate your Sacred Circle. Claim your Self as the Warrior as you step forward.

1. Activate the four directions: first the South, West, North, and finally the East. You will need your tobacco. (I always liken this process to turning on a light switch in a room; as you present your Self to each direction there is an activation that takes place within that direction. When you complete all four directions your whole circle is lit up.)

2. Go to the South direction and present your Self, opening up to the elements of the South. Address the elements: "Elements of the South I call you forward." (You can say this aloud or just think it.)

3. Take a pinch of tobacco, hold it to your heart, wait until you feel some connection within your heart, and then present it with your hand upward. Wait until you feel that you are being received in some way and then place it on the South stone.

4. Do the same with each direction, moving in a clockwise direction.
5. Move to your central stone. Here, you connect to Great Spirit, asking for help, asking to be shown the way, asking to receive the teaching. Use your tobacco, holding it to your heart, holding it up to connect to the Great Spirit, and downward to the Earth to the Earth Mother, calling to Father Sun, Mother Moon, the Grandmothers, and Grandfathers, honoring the above and below worlds, and then calling to the Ancestors. You call these energies forward to support you in your quest. You then place the tobacco on the central stone in thanks for all that you are about to receive. Note: The Ancestors are all those who have walked this path before you and all of those who have forged this path in order for you to move forward more easily on your path.

The above worlds includes the Star energies within the Galaxy; the below worlds includes the mineral kingdom and all energies beneath the Earth.

Working Within Your Medicine Circle

Let go of all concepts and just Be.

1. Go to the central stone and open up a prayer to Great Spirit, Mother Earth, Father Sun, the Grandmothers, the Grandfathers, and the Ancestors. Call them forward to be with you at this time and bring the teachings to you.
2. Open up with a prayer asking to be shown the way. Ask for the help you need at this time. You come forward in humbleness, not knowing, and just being open to receive.
3. Use your drum or rattle when opening your connection. Remember your drum or rattle creates the connection, the opening.
4. Each direction within your Medicine Wheel holds certain qualities for you, but it is important to first present your Self to each direction. Beginning in the South, using either your rattle or drum, sit on the earth or stand as you rattle or drum to that direction. The elements connected to the South will respond to you. You may have a feeling to stop and be still, meditating quietly with those elements in that direction.
5. Connect in the same way with the West, North, and East directions.
6. Feel where you need to be within your circle. You may be pulled to a certain direction or even to the central place. You may just feel like lying down on the earth to receive. Use your drum or

rattle in whatever direction calls to you. This will expand your connection. Or it may feel right just to sit in that direction and just be with the elements. You can trust your feeling here. What does this direction have to show you? What message does it bring to you? It is normal to feel a deeper connection to one particular direction than others. It is important to honor that calling and spend time in that particular direction.

Leaving Your Medicine Circle

Always leave through your East doorway. Pick up your central stone in the doorway, walk through, and then close the doorway by replacing your stone behind you. Never just walk over your stones. You need to leave your circle consciously, giving thanks to Great Spirit and the four directions for the teaching.

If you are not going to return to use your medicine circle it is important to take your circle apart. Replace your stones where you found them and leave some tobacco on the earth in thanks for all that you received.

The Elements of Each Direction

South

- **Color:** red
- **Time of day:** noon
- **Season:** middle of summer
- **Element:** fire
- **Teaching:** Place of the child, brings you back to innocence. Place of the birthing of your creativity. Place of sexuality, place of passion.
- **Power animals:** the snake, the scorpion (all land reptiles).
- **Action:** Transmutation through the bite. Completion of the South is the Fire Ceremony, which marks our movement toward the East.

The South opens up a movement to erase personal history, which means to release the energy of past traumas that affects your life today. The South is about personal healing.

West

- **Color:** black
- **Time of day:** sunset
- **Season:** autumn
- **Element:** water
- **Teaching:** The work is to seek the qualities of introspection and intuition through a deep inner humbleness for meeting oneself.
- **Power animals:** otter, whale, dolphins, beaver, and turtle (all water creatures)
- **Action:** The West relates to cultural healing. This is all the belief systems you have chosen to take on through the teachings of your particular family.

North

- **Color:** white
- **Time of day:** midnight
- **Season:** middle of winter
- **Element:** earth
- **Teaching:** The place of death. To "face your death and make death your ally"; to re-make your deep connection to Mother Earth and the Elements.
- **Power animals:** wolf, horse, bear, coyote (all four legged)
- **Action:** Deep introspection by hibernation, grounding in wisdom manifesting your new Self and your vision in the material plane, committing yourself to assuming authority over your life, your Self, and your circle.

East

- **Color:** yellow
- **Time of day:** sunrise
- **Season:** spring
- **Element:** air
- **Teaching:** The work is to seek Vision, Illumination, and understanding of Truth. Your work includes:
    - Mother Nature teaches you.
    - Re-union to elemental forces.

- • Ceremony of re-birth to your true parents, Mother Earth and Father Sun.
- • **Power animals:** eagle, all winged messengers, the crow that brings the energy of the shape-shifter
- • **Action:** illumination, re-birth

~~~

Beloved Ones,

We greet you. So much is taking place on your planet right now. You are beginning to move into some new realms of understanding; realms where you are aligning to truth, where you are remembering. It is so exciting to witness you as you awaken, as you step forward in understanding.

Do not hesitate to move forward. Some things will make no sense at all to you, but don't let that stop your forward rhythm. Trust the feeling of rightness in the step, and keep dancing through the waves of your life.

We are with you. We salute you. We love you.

Blessings,
The Pleiadians

~~~

6

Aligning to Your Mission, Fulfilling Your Destiny

As you take your place to fulfill your mission on this earth plane during this New Dawning time, you will receive knowledge and understanding, along with a certain nutrition that will feed you. This is the direct energy from the Principles for Living to which you are beginning to re-align.

Nothing is separate. All life force within the Universe is linked by the common element of the God Consciousness that resides within each life force, and part of this common element is birthed by the sacred alignment to the Principles for Living. This journey is for your divine aspect to be unveiled to your Self in this lifetime. Yes, you have your human aspect. There is space for you to experience your human element and at the same time unveil the sacred part of your Self. It is part of your destiny to step forward and be part of a powerful momentum that is happening on your planet. It is part of your mission to take your place, play your part, and re-align back to the living principles so that you can remember and reunite with your Self.

The Grand Plan includes you working in alignment with the Galactic Council, the Spiritual realms, the alien energies, and all life force groups throughout the Universe. You have a part to play within this Grand Plan, and it is time for you to consciously take your place. Every human being on this earth plane, regardless of what they are doing or who they are, has made a pre-agreement to be here at this time. It does not matter whether you are consciously awake or not. What matters is that you all said yes to being here, and to realize that each one of you has a part to play. Those of you who are awake and have been working on your own spiritual path will have a greater role to play right now within the Universe.

It is essential to simply let go. Allow yourself to be moved within to a very different aspect of your Self, which will birth a new wave of light on your earth plane. This wave of light will gather in force as each one of you consciously allows this light to birth through you. This wave of light is going to set in motion a gathering momentum within the dimensional character of your planet, so that a powerful anchoring of a multi-dimensional energy can become a permanent aspect of your planet Earth.

There are many of you Light Workers, Healers, Star beings, and other alliance energies here on the earth plane in human form. Many of you have made pre-agreements to fulfill the destiny of your earth plane and, at the same time, to fulfill your own destiny of transformation and transmutation. A powerful transmutation is going to take place within the cells of every human being that is awake. You can hold that truth and feel that truth through your heart center. Your own heart recognizes this truth and is waiting to begin this transmutation.

This new wave of light that will birth through each of your heart cells will be a like a flame igniting through the cell as you receive this multi-dimensional force that will transmute your heart. The transmutation of each heart cell will create a perfect womb to hold the frequency of your true loving element of unconditional love.

Through this tremendous force of love flowing on to the planet, through you and many others, there will be a new creation made possible through the transformation of the frequency on your planet. This energetic structure is being created to anchor a series of sacred births on your planet.

Unconditional love, as it births through the heart cells, will open up a series of transformational portals within the earth plane, which will create a revolution within your planet. These portals will channel in the full birth of the New Dawning energy. Your heart center will be like a full receiving station once it is linked to these light portals. Know that through the birthing of a portal in your own heart you have a direct connection to these transformational portals.

You will receive through your heart and then naturally transmit this energy outward across the earth plane. This will birth a pathway of energy, making it possible for many others to follow the path themselves, creating an unveiling of truth to all who are ready. These portals of light are aligned to the Collective Consciousness; those of you who are awake will birth yourselves through this sacred connection to the Principles for Living. As a group you are pre-destined to anchor the New Dawning era on to the earth plane.

It is up to those of you living on this earth plane, as part of your destiny, to be instrumental in this birthing within the earth plane. WE are here to assist you; YOU as are here to anchor and birth your planet dimensionally. This is what you have come here to do!

Within the Grand Plan the spiritual realms—the Masters, Light beings, and Angels—are working with people on the earth plane to bring them to a certain level of awakening or alignment though their channels or whatever medium they are working with to fulfill this mission. The spiritual realms are also working within the energetic field of the earth plane and assisting in anchoring energetic grids and alignments within the earth itself, and some are working with those individual people or groups who are setting up energetic grids.

The Pleiadians are working with groups on the earth plane, and also channeling with individuals to create a set of alignments and light initiation processes for human beings. This is all written in the Grand Plan, and each group is coming in and playing its part. They are all part of the Oneness, part of a telepathic communion system to support you in completing this transition.

Another piece of the Grand Plan is the crop circles coming into their full roles for the first time on the earth plane, which will be more fully revealed in Chapter 8. They are aligning to all the megalith sites on the planet. The crop circles are being re-aligned back to their original pure state, re-activating the energy of the ancient teachings and knowledge that they originally held. These sacred energies are anchoring now through the earth plane.

There are energetic lines forming between the crop circles and the megalith sites around our earth plane. This is creating a sacred webbing, assisting with the anchoring of many dimensional grids that are supporting the transformation of our planet. This webbing will hold energetic openings in readiness for the portals of light to anchor on the earth plane.

As you can see, each light force group is playing its part within the Grand Plan. Connected through a mutual telepathic communion the Pleiadians and the spiritual realms are working side-by-side, aligned on higher dimensional levels within the sacred communion with the Galactic Council.

The Galactic Council is playing a crucial role. They hold a pure consciousness of light, and they are working with certain energetic and dimensional principles to align matter with their consciousness. They are able to keep objects in balance on a dimensional level as this birthing is taking place on the earth plane. At the same time, they hold all sacred alignments within a communion within the Oneness.

There is a divine orchestration. Of course you are here in your human element, sometimes with the ego, sometimes within your more expanded states and making your way. You are waking up and re-aligning to Self with all of this support.

You need to have some understanding of what is taking place, and I know this description is inadequate. Your language cannot fully hold the truth of all that is taking place. However, I have to create a picture for you to understand what is happening now and what is coming, in part to explain your place and your next steps so you can say, *Okay, I'm going to take another step today for my awakening.* So be it!

Template Energy

Those of you who are ready are being called to create a Template Energy that will be anchored onto the earth plane. This Template Energy will be utilized within the Grand Plan. By consciously activating your Template, you will be activating a piece of your sacred aspect onto the earth plane and simultaneously realigning back to the Principles for Living. The Template Energy is pure dimensional space that is capable of containing your light form energy. This is your divine light aspect that remains connected to you as you anchor the Template on the earth plane where it is utilized to support the birthing of the new dimensional energies on the earth plane.

Anchoring your Template is giving you access to your divine light, to which you could not align previously. The Template gives you an opportunity and opens a doorway for you to work directly within your divine light pathway. It's almost as though you are bathed in this light of your Self for a rapid transformation, enabling you to carry a higher level of your own consciousness of light in the cells of your body. Then you will act as a transmitter for the planet and for other people as you go through this transmutation within your heart cells.

Activating your Template allows you to evolve to another level of consciousness of your Self, you birthing you. You accelerate your birthing process through the activation of your Template. As you anchor your Template there is the natural process of opening into a conscious alignment with the Galactic Council.

You will be linked into this communion, which accelerates your birthing process, because it takes you within a sacred flow that is held in the Universe. A new clarity opens up as you join the family of light. You will enter a higher dimensional telepathic space, and participate and grow through the higher truths transmitted in this telepathic arena.

One player is not more important that the other. Everyone works toward the collective Grand Plan, and everyone is playing his or her full role. The sacred design is for all of you to return back to your original places within the Universal Consciousness. As you take up your conscious connection to your place within the Universal Grid, the whole (which is the Universal Consciousness) becomes complete once again.

Anchoring your Template can be likened to setting off on a raft in rapids, not sure how to navigate yourself. Let go, open to trust. You may not be ready for this step, and that is okay. Just know you can come back to these processes at any time for this activation when you feel ready.

I have spent the last 25 years taking my next step and letting go. It has been a wonderful, fulfilling journey and I have felt blessed and taken care of each step of the way. At times I have felt overwhelmed, and this was caused by my ego assessment of an unfamiliar experience taking place within me as I transformed. As I came back into my heart I was able to let go; being overwhelmed changed into a feeling of peace.

You now have a choice: You can skip to the next chapter, and when it feels right you can come back and activate your Template Energy.

Steps to Activate Your Template

It is important to understand that, at the moment you have completed the activation of your Template, you will have a direct alignment to the Galactic Council. What does that mean? It means that you will be held within a telepathic communion and overseen by them as an active part of the Collective Consciousness. They will hold you in a more complete way because you have aligned consciously to your divine aspect.

To begin, make sure you have your Template page in front of you. You need to align to the two columns of symbols with both hands and see all the symbols on both columns. Look at the Template shown in Diagram F on page 79. You can photocopy this page and enlarge it, which will help you have full access to the page during your awakening process. It will support you in aligning to the two columns more easily.

You will need your sacred sound: ANAE EE TAH. Remember: Your frequency of the sacred sound is unique; it is recognized within the Universe. Let go and allow this birthing energy through you.

1st Process

Audio file: Chapter 6
Audio file #1

1. Bring the palms of your hands together at the heart center (on the sternum line). Bring your Conscious Awareness to the connection point where the palms meet and take a Conscious Breath.

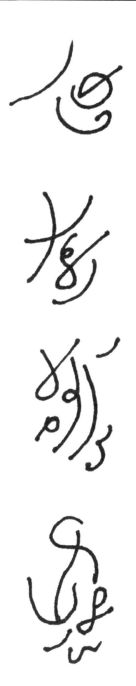

Diagram F

Let go and open into an alignment. You are going to continue to build an alignment core within you.

2. Use your sacred sound through your core alignment: ANAE EE TAH. Feel how your core alignment transforms through your sacred sound. Let go; allow the transformation.

3. Bring your Conscious Awareness to your Template page. Slowly bring each hand from your core alignment position to line up with each individual column of symbols so that your left hand aligns with the left column and the right hand lines up with the right column.

4. Bring your full consciousness into the columns and feel how your hands begin to anchor/align with each column. Let go and just allow your experience to fully build.

5. When you feel ready you are going to use the sacred sound ANAE EE TAH. This will begin the anchoring of your Template Energy. Just let go, and be open to the download of energy moving through you and new connections of light being given to you.

6. When you are complete, bring the palms of your hands back to the core position. Allow the full integration through your core. Just let go and allow a transitional energy to move through your core alignment.

Remember: Each time you breathe and let go, another level of re-alignment can take place within you.

2nd Process

Audio file: Chapter 6
Audio File #2

Thought code: SUN EE SHAH. Note: This is not a sound; it is sent by the mind and placed within the telepathic center.

Lie on the floor or earth. Note: If you cannot lie down, you can sit in a chair.

1. The palms of your hands need to be facing upward toward the sky, hands placed by your side. Bring your consciousness into each palm of your hand. Take a Conscious Breath and let go.

2. Bring your right hand up and open into your telepathic center. Take the time to fully open into your telepathic center before you move on.

3. Use the thought code SUN EE SHAH. You are going to place this into your telepathic center. This thought code is going to create

an expanded communion connection for you to access higher dimensional communications.

4.   Let go and breathe the energy of the opening. Allow the transfer of energy to expand through your telepathic center.

5.   Use the thought code SUN EE SHAH. Allow another level of the energetic transfer. Just let go and allow this experience.

6.   Bring your right hand down to close off your telepathic center. Bring the palms of your hands facing upward, and both hands by your sides. Bring your Conscious Awareness into your palms, use the Conscious Breath, and let go. Open up the re-alignment through the cells of your body.

7.   Use the sacred sound ANAE EE TAH. As you do this each cell in your body will go through a re-alignment process. Use the sound until your feel fully integrated.

3rd Process: Working With Your Activated Template

Audio file: Chapter 6
Audio File #3

You have now activated your Template. It is important for you to be conscious of your telepathic openings that will give you a new perspective energetically. Be aware that you will be given a higher access to the dimensional codes that exist within the Universe in order to activate your light signature. Your light signature is the aspect of your light that has anchored through your Template.

You can work with your light signature through the use of these dimensional codes that create alignments for you. You are the only one who has access to your own light signature.

How to Work With Your Dimensional Codes

1.   You will need to work within your expanded telepathic center to work with your new dimensional codes. Open up your right hand and access your telepathic center. Make sure you are fully expanded within your telepathic center.

2.   Bring both hands together to form a triangle. See Diagram G on the following page, which shows this hand position. Note: The index fingers are connected. With the thumb they come together at the base to form a triangle.

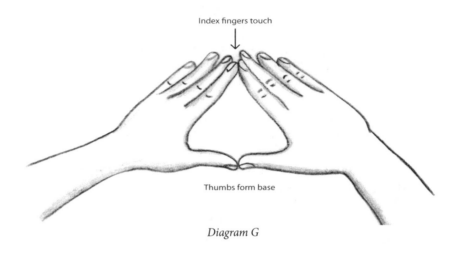

Index fingers touch

Thumbs form base

Diagram G

3. Bring your Conscious Awareness into the doorway of the tri-
    angle; just breathe and let go. Take your time to feel an opening
    within the doorway. Now take your consciousness deeper into
    the triangle. Take a breath and let go. Here you begin to align to
    your dimensional codes. Keep receiving these codes and let go.
4. Now bring your full consciousness out of the doorway and come
    into your telepathic center. It is still open. Just bring your con-
    sciousness into your third eye area and you will be brought fully
    into your telepathic center. You carry the dimensional codes with
    you into this space.
5. Use the thought code SUN EE SHAH. Place it within your tele-
    pathic center. You begin to receive aspects of your light signature
    from your anchored template. You need to work with the levels
    of your light signature by integrating with your Conscious Breath
    and then letting go.

By activating your light signature you will be energetically moved and
aligned more deeply into the higher dimensional realms. As this activation
takes place your light frequency will begin to transmit outward into the Universal Grid. It is here on the Grid that you will re-anchor your light placement.
Your light placement within the Grid has been waiting for this signal from the
activation of your light signature. As your light signature pulsates through the
Universe there is recognition by the universal community as it activates your
place on the Grid. It is another step of your return home. Know that you can

develop and expand dimensional aspects of your light signature as you re-journey with this audio file. This process will continue to anchor you in your placement.

You may experience some disorientation through the activation of your light signature. This is because you are re-aligning to new dimensional settings within your Self. Don't try to return to what you have known; just let go and allow your transformation. Call the energies forward for support and allow this re-birthing.

~~~

Beloved Ones,

We greet you and in this moment of time we ask you to open up to the energies that are being held for you now. Now is the time to step forward to receive many gifts. These gifts are yours by divine birthright, and they are being made available to you because you need them.

You have said yes to being here at this time. You have said yes to a journey of divine proportions so that you take your place within the Collective Consciousness, the Oneness. You have a place within the Oneness. To claim this place consciously is so essential at this time.

As you claim your place on a conscious level a door can open and you can walk through this doorway. We hold this doorway open with tremendous love and respect for all that you are in this moment. Know that you are "perfectly imperfect" in your human-ness. There is nothing that you need to change about yourself in order to be received within this light wheel on the Universal Grid.

Take a breath and claim yourself within your human-ness. Hold your Self with love and deep appreciation for your journey and all that you have lived up to this point in.

Our role is to bring the fifth-dimensional energy of unconditional love to each one of you as you fulfill your destiny. We are here to assist, simply to hold the love. Be still and know the truth of this within your heart. Walk through the doorway and take your place.

Blessings,
The Pleiadians

~~~

7

Building Your Telepathic Communion
With Life Force Groups

Communicating with all life force groups within the Collective Consciousness ends another level of separation within your Self. There are many levels of communion possible within the multi-dimensional spaces you will navigate. Each dimensional aspect that you open into allows another level of separation within you to drop away.

You have spent lifetimes caught up in a place of powerlessness through the illusion of the third-dimensional world, keeping your Self separated from the rest of the Universe. You have played a passive role by meditating and waiting to be given information or shown the answers.

This state of waiting has now ended, because the veils of illusion are lifting on your planet. With the veils lifting you can now directly access the universal community, and in doing this through Conscious Choice, you naturally re-align to the Principles for Living. Your place within the Collective Consciousness is so much more than the limited version you have of your Self. Through your direct experience of this ability to telepathically communicate with all life force groups, you will quickly move into an experience of empowerment within your Self.

Only through your heart connection are you going to comprehend the enormity of this truth and anchor the truth of this within the consciousness of each heart cell.

However, each time that you do hold this truth within your heart, even for one moment, there will be an acceleration within you, a quickening, and you will experience an exhilaration within the cells of your heart. This is because you are anchoring into a truth within the moment, and in that moment you step outside the illusion that has been holding you in place for lifetimes. You move your dimensional perception.

Enough with the third-dimensional illusions that have held you within the confines of planet Earth for lifetimes! Enough with the restrictions that you have placed on yourself, keeping you small and insignificant. You have been held within the illusion of the third dimension by the constraints of time, the limitations of believing in *lack*, and the disconnection to our true spiritual nature of being a creator.

Now is the time to fly through a timeless place, to be received and acknowledged by your Self for all that you are in your brilliance and to once again feel the love and connections that feed and nourish your spirit through the reconnection to all life force energies within the Universal realms.

Through the activation of your crystalline energy, the activation of your telepathic center, and the possible anchoring of your Template Energy, you can open up to a communication within the Universal realms and begin exploring your true essence. Know that it is enough to just be open to the possibility that these multi-dimensional aspects of Self exist, and that these life force energies actually exist.

As you allow yourself to open to these possibilities, and when your thoughts align to this truth, a doorway opens for you. You are still human, and being human is part of your process. Appreciate the dynamic of your ego within your process. Your relationship to your ego needs to be developed so that there is a transformative dynamic taking place based on love, compassion, and patience. This is part of your journey to integrate the human ego by creating a direct link through your heart, moving from a third-dimensional ego-based relationship to a fourth/fifth-dimensional connection through the heart.

There are many aspects of your Self to explore and understand within this multi-dimensional aspect, knowing that within these levels are vast experiences for you to digest within this journey. There are many different reunion alliances that will support you in remembering key truths and being able to fully integrate these truths.

You are being asked to see this as a multi-layered journey, and to allow your Self to exist within levels of experiences as you have them. Do not try to control or maneuver your experiences. Allow a natural re-birthing process to emerge within you. Let go and take this in: There is nothing to do. There is nothing to try to do. Simply open to experiencing what is in front of you and let go. There may be moments within your journey when you will find it hard to receive what is being presented to you. Try not to work it out in your ego mind. Just know that all will unfold and you will come to truth as you move forward when the time is right.

I remember when I had my first experience with the Pleiadian ship. I turned a corner into a field and there in front of me was this huge spaceship. At that time I didn't believe in aliens and spaceships. Then a group of Pleiadians began walking toward me, telepathically reminding me of my pre-agreement to act as a Pleiadian Ambassador here on the earth plane. My whole world felt as though it was going to shatter.

In that moment I came back into my full memory of everything I had pre-agreed to complete in this lifetime. It's as though I went back in time to the point just before I came into this world and had a full memory of my full essence. In that moment I recognized my Pleiadian family before me and moved back into the experience of my Pleiadian heritage.

It was an extreme moment of transformation and really too much to even comprehend. The most difficult thing for me was that I could not ignore the experience. It was too extreme. It took me many months to come to terms with who I was, and what I was to do. I went into a separated state for a while, until I came to a truth: The Pleiadians are part of the Oneness, a part of the God consciousness. With this understanding I could move forward into my complete mission. I needed to take my time to accept what the truth was and then I needed to take my time in integrating my powerful experience. I could not move forward until I had fully allowed my human process. Remember: You can take your time to allow all aspects of you to integrate the truths as they are unveiled before you.

Understand that "home" is a concept of the human ego. You need to be willing to let go of all limited concepts, the ego attachment, and the constant assessment that dialogue creates. Your ego mind holds a limited energetic form of home. Your true home has no limitations, no boundaries. It is vast and beautiful, with space to hold all multi-dimensional aspects of you, of Self.

You will need to set yourself free of concepts of what this journey will be, what it will look like, or how it will feel. Come with no expectations and just allow the experience to take place within your heart. The Pleiadians have helpful, step-by-step processes to support you as you open into your heart to have your full multi-dimensional experiences.

There are many levels to this journey and they all begin in your heart. There is a place within your heart cells that has the memory of home. If that memory feels too painful to tolerate, I ask you to take a breath and choose to allow yourself to remember, even if it causes you pain. You need to meet this pain, this emotion, to come back to your place of home. This ends an aspect of the separation so that you can move into the truth of your own journey back to Self. This pain around home has been created through a misperception of circumstances by the ego mind. Through this remembering you will come into a peaceful place in which you can continue forward on your mission. The pain needs to be transmuted through your heart.

It is necessary to allow yourself to move past the place of separation because this will give you access to a frequency of home, almost like dialing a phone number and connecting you. This frequency of home, however, is so much more than a phone number. It is more like an energetic setting that links you into a light flow that takes you to your home connections. It is essential that you anchor this realignment through your heart. This will build a strong base setting for you to move and experience all the multi-dimensional states of your Self, so you can journey and re-align back to a true experience and connection to home. It is an important jumping-off point for you.

You need this base setting in order to take the momentous leap into beginning to connect to other life force energy groups within the Universe. You are being asked to take your place and play your part. This is only possible by first anchoring "home."

To find the dimensional area within your heart that has the memory of home is not a difficult thing. We will be working together, and once you have an anchoring of these settings within your heart space, you will begin to journey through dimensional spaces within your heart and open into multi-dimensional energetic experiences.

Through one of the processes channeled by the Pleiadians, you will be working within a dimensional aspect of your heart, as well as aligning to your telepathic center. The synergy of these two sacred spaces within you makes it possible for you to move dimensionally into aspects of your Self, where you can navigate yourself home. This aspect of your Self aligns through the combined energies of your heart and telepathic communion center. Anchoring to home will bring about many powerful changes within you. Your sense of Self will transform and you will begin to align to your personal signature.

Once again, you are on a self-birthing journey—you birthing you. This was the way you were meant to come back home. Know that you will not be doing this alone. There will be supports in place, energetic alliances that you have pre-agreed to have come and assist you in your homecoming. You have many alliances to open into before you can become an effective energetic element and fully take your place. It is only with your connection to home that you can play a more active role with other life force groups within the Universe.

The plan has always been that, in this lifetime, you would have your human experience and move into a conscious awakening experience with your divine aspect, returning to Self.

Finding the Memory of Home/Anchoring Home

Audio file: Chapter 7
Audio file #1

Let's look at the energetic process that will give you access to the dimensional area within the heart that holds the memory of home.

1. Bring the palms of your hands to hold your entire heart space. Understand that your entire heart space is your full physical chest area and an area beyond the physical body. When you hold your full chest area with both palms you are interconnecting through the full space of the heart, including the many multi-dimensional aspects of your heart. As you hold your heart center, open up to this multi-dimensional area. Claim all aspects of its multi-dimensionality, even if you are on an ego level unaware of these existing spaces.

    This is a powerful step that you take when you acknowledge the existence of these aspects of your heart. There is a certain activation that begins to take place, an awakening. Remember: It has been at least one lifetime since you worked within these dimensional spaces within your heart.

2. Close your eyes and bring your Conscious Awareness into your heart center. Allow your consciousness to scan the full space. It might take you fully outside your physical frame. You are looking for an opening. Whether you sense it, feel it, or see it, it is important not to engage the mind. Just let go and allow it. Your heart will support you in finding the opening.

3. When you detect the opening bring your Conscious Awareness to just touch the opening. When you touch the opening your heart will respond in some way by expanding, vibrating, pulsing, heating, or moving in patterns. Open into the experience.

4. When your heart has responded you will use a sacred sound: ANAE SHEAN. Your unique frequency within this sound will be recognized and you will be drawn into the opening in this dimensional setting. Use the sound ANAE SHEAN until you become one with the dimensional energy.

5. Let go and open your consciousness into this dimensional space. Breathe and open fully into these energies. There is a thought code that brings you into your memory of home, which links you. Let go and send the thought code AE NAH. Remember: You place the code within this space.

6. Wait for a response within the area. You will feel a veil begin to lift. You may just experience an expansion of light or shifting of energy as this happens. Send the thought code AE NAH as the veil lifts on another level. It is almost like a light coming on or the sun beginning to show its light just on the horizon. Use the thought code AE NAH once more. Feel the energy within the space open as the light intensifies.

7. Keep opening to your energy of home as it builds and comes toward you, greeting you within the building light. Let go and breathe.

8. Claim your energy of home by anchoring this dimensional space. You do this by bringing your right hand upward and open the thumb outward. Look at Diagram H, which shows hand position. Feel yourself being received as you bring your right hand up. You are acknowledging this energy of home and you are being acknowledged.

   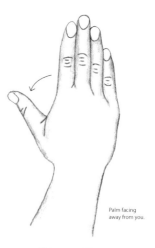

   Palm facing away from you.

   Diagram H

   It may be a telepathic communion connection, so allow an opening through your heart center to birth in this moment. Allow this dimensional birthing experience through you, breathe and let go. It will support this dimensional birth through your heart.

9. Bring your full consciousness into your hand position again and let go. You need to allow the full anchoring to take place. Take the time you need to complete the anchoring before you bring your hand position down.

   Note: This hand position plays the role of a dimensional bookmark as well as a dimensional anchor, so that you are able to come back to your home energy when you need to.

10. Bring your hand position down and come back to your full heart space with both hands on your chest. Bring your Conscious Awareness into your full heart space. Breathe and let go into the full dimensional opening within your heart.

Connecting to Life Force Groups Consciously

Audio file: Chapter 7
Audio file #2

There is a certain recipe, with specific steps to be taken, that enables you to consciously connect with any life force group within the Universe. You have already created an anchoring within your multi-dimensional heart and "book-marked" your position of home within your heart space with your hand position. This is going to allow you to access your connection to home, and you will build that connection each time you access it. You will also use it to create a strong base setting to journey within the Universe.

You are now ready to take your next step toward connecting and opening into a sacred communion with other life force groups within the Universe. You are going to access multi-dimensional aspects of your Self as you do this. This is your Self discovery!

Creating Your Base Setting

1. Bring the palms of your hands together at the center of your heart line (at the sternum). Bring your Conscious Awareness to where the palms meet and take a Conscious Breath. Let go and move into the alignment, the opening. Feel the opening of your core. You may feel heat, tingling, vibration, calmness—let go and be with your experience. You need to take your time building this core space. You are going to need a strong core birthed to support your traveling through the dimensional settings.

   With each Conscious Breath you let go. The "letting go" action further establishes your core. Feel your core anchoring down into the earth, like roots of a tree. Keep letting go and allow the full expression of your core. You may feel, see, or sense your core; it may be subtle or strong. It is irrelevant how it presents itself.

2. Bring your right hand up to open your telepathic center. Bring your full Conscious Awareness to your hand position and use the Conscious Breath. Feel the opening of the doorway and enter the

space. Breathe and let go into the doorway, and feel the energy expand within the space. Move within the space and follow the bridge, pathway, or line that connects you into your telepathic center. Allow your experience.

Note: You are now going to dimensionally expand your telepathic center. You are ready for this. You need a different dimensional setting to be established within your telepathic center in order to create the correct synergy for your base setting between your telepathic center and your bookmarked position of home within your heart space.

3. Fill your telepathic center with your Conscious Awareness. Use the Conscious Breath and let go into the full space. Allow the full expression of the birth, letting go.

    You are going to place a thought code into your telepathic center. This will create a dimensional expansion. You may experience your telepathic center going through a metamorphosis. During this birthing process you must allow the full expression that is created through the use of the thought code within your center. Place the thought code SUN EE SHAH. Breathe and let go as you move into the transformation that is taking place. You will place the thought code three times. Each time, allow for the full integration and movement within your telepathic center. This expansion will allow you to create expanded communion connections, enabling you to access higher dimensional communications within the Universe.

4. Open up your hand position that links you into home. Bring your full Conscious Awareness within the energy of that hand position. This is your bookmark of home. Allow your telepathic opening to move into the hand position and to your full connection to the place of home. You may experience an essence from home bringing their connection to your hand. Your telepathic center is open, so you can allow an expanded connection to take place.

    Just let go and allow your experience through this telepathic communion. Feel the full synergy between your telepathic center and home. This connection is being forged right now. Your base setting is being created.

5. When this connection feels complete bring your right hand down. Come back to your core position with the palms of both

hands together at the center of your heart line. Bring all of your Conscious Awareness into your core and integrate this new dimensional energy through your core by using your Conscious Breath. Make sure that all of your Conscious Awareness meets through your core. Become aware of how your core has expanded with this new birthed aspect of light.

Connecting to Life Force Groups Within the Universe

Audio file: Chapter 7
Audio file #3

You now have your base setting established. This means that you can move forward and work directly with any life force group with whom you feel a connection.

Realize that by establishing your base setting you are now able to integrate multi-dimensional aspects of your sacred Self. It is essential that you remain open throughout these multi-dimensional experiences, understanding that the ego has no reference point within these spaces. Choose to be in a space of acceptance of your varied experiences, *witnessing* rather than commenting or negating.

Base Setting

Your base setting is the sacred synergy of your expanded telepathic center and your bookmark position of home. The hand position is shown in Diagram H.

1. Begin by anchoring through your core. Bring the palms of your hands together at the center of your heart line. Bring your Conscious Awareness to the connecting palms and feel the opening and expression of your core. Allow it to build and anchor into the earth, like roots of a tree. You need a strong core established in order to move through the dimensional spaces. It will allow you to travel dimensionally and stay balanced.

2. You will activate your base setting by bringing your right hand upward with your thumb held out away from your four fingers (see Diagram H).

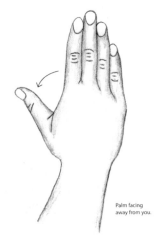

Palm facing away from you.

Diagram H

Bring your full Conscious Awareness into your hand position and enter into the doorway. Breathe and let go into the energy, anchoring your Self within the synergy connection. You become a part of the synergy that is present and open to the Oneness that exists here. Take your time establishing this connection. Keep bringing your Conscious Awareness into the space and deepening your connection.

3. This connection brings you into the dimensional settings within the Collective Consciousness. To enter this space you use a sound that brings your unique frequency forward, and it is recognized throughout this space. A doorway opens to take you within the flow that exists here, and you begin to take your place. Use the sound EE SHAH TAH, but add as many sounds as you need until you feel yourself moving into your place within the dimensional flow. Let go and allow your experience. Feel yourself being received and celebrated.

4. When you are ready to open to a specific energetic alliance, bring your Conscious Awareness fully into your hand position. You immediately open into the full expansion of your telepathic communion center. Continue to align with the energy within your hand. You will feel a connecting energy meeting you within the alignment to your hand. Open and fully experience the communion.

5. When you choose to complete this connection, bring your right hand down. Come back to your core position with both palms coming together at your heart center. You need to integrate through your core fully, making sure that all parts of your consciousness are back within the core space before you are complete.

Let go and use the Conscious Breath. There has been a transformation within your energetic field and cells of your body. Allow the natural forces to support you in integrating these expanded energies. Lie or sit on the earth.

As you take this step of connecting to another alliance energy through telepathic communion know that you take a huge step forward within your Self. Through this sacred communion there is a metamorphosis that takes place within your heart cells from the exchange of love that is held within the communion act. Each time you choose the form of telepathic communion there will be this ongoing transformation. Honor your Self for this powerful step!

~~~

Beloved Ones,

We greet you with love. Understand that as you step forward into your trans-formation every cell in your body will align to a new truth. This allows the illusion to drop away and the cells in your body, in your moment of choosing, can transform and re-align.

It only takes one moment of choosing for true transformation to take place. To consciously choose to open and trust and receive is all that it takes for your change. The doors are wide open for you now. Choose and let go. Move into the energy of the opening in front of you. This alignment will bring you home to your self. We witness you.

With love,
The Pleiadians

~~~

8

Crop Circles

Beloved Ones,

You are being gently guided from one world to another, and this is a process of purpose, bringing you into an alignment with the Truth. What a gift you are experiencing. Understand that you are part of the gift that is unfolding now.
Blessings,
The Pleiadians

~~~

Crop circles are formations that are usually found in grain crops. They were created by the Pleiadians. They are birthed through a high frequency of light sound and are created in sacred patterns, energetically designed specifically to assist us in this New Dawning time. Through a sacred webbing that the crop circles are weaving, there is a new network of light grid lines and energetic vortexes opening up on the earth plane. This new avenue of light is being anchored on to planet Earth in order for each one of you to have an accelerated opportunity to move forward into your enlightenment process at this time. The formation of this energetic network is designed to support the change of your planet evolving to fourth/fifth-dimensional consciousness. The crop circles were always meant to come into their fully awakened state and play a major role in this profound dynamic evolution of the Earth at this time.

Through time, the crop circles have been strategically placed on the planet in preparation for this New Dawning era. Their multi-dimensional, geometrical forms carry sacred designs that contain ancient knowledge to be accessed and utilized. They hold awakening codes for all human beings. They hold the platform for the full transformation of the Earth and all human beings to awaken, and they hold the whole energetic map of the completed form of this New Dawning era.

There are dimensional layers of circles of light within each crop circle. Within each layer there are intricate geometrical patterns that make up the individual circles. All crop circles interact with each other and create a powerful and dynamic synergy that births a force of light, which creates a portal through which the Collective Consciousness is channeled. This sets the stage for all life force within the earth plane to birth into a new potential for regeneration.

The sacred crop circles' light holds a pure state of truth that impacts the awakening of the earth plane to new realms. There are a number of dimensional blueprint settings within the crop circles that have sacred texts containing the activating blueprints for your awakening and transformation. Through these dimensional blueprint settings individual ancestral alliances are forged with certain life force groups within the Universe, re-uniting those pre-agreement energetic alliances between some human beings and those from the light realms within the Collective Consciousness.

The crop circles are bringing a dynamic awakening to you and the earth plane as they move into their full potential. Everything is in readiness for them to transmit and open levels of dimensional energies required for the rapid transformation of consciousness on planet Earth. They hold the doorways open for you to begin the re-alignment back to the sacred Principles for Living. As these Living Principles are activated a new dimensional frequency is anchored on the earth plane. Through this frequency the crop circles begin to play a significant role by creating a series of re-alignments to all the sacred megalith sites on the planet. All megalith sites are made from stone. Megalith sites are sacred sites such as Stonehenge and the Great Pyramids. Part of the crop circles' energetic purpose is to realign all the megalithic sites back to the original, pure, sacred form that they held when they first birthed onto the earth plane. There is a pure energy of consciousness that has opened through each sacred megalith form, for the purpose of holding a base of light through the sacred webbing in support of the ongoing transformation of you and the planet.

The crop circles act as a catalyst by opening up a series of light force lines, creating a series of energetic grid lines between themselves and all the megaliths sites. Picture this energetic webbing being formed around your planet as all the crop circles and all the megalith sites interconnect. This transformational net acts as a womb for the earth's dimensional and physical changes, creating an ongoing stability for the new dimensional openings to birth on to the earth plane. This dimensional womb also gives support for you to evolve into a new level of your essence through the transformational birthing of your crystalline structure.

The crop circles are going to continue to expand and transmit light frequencies outward, aligning the earth, and playing a part in the awakening of each one of you as you birth and redefine yourselves during these changing times. There is an element of sacred geometry within the crop circles that is activating the Stargates within the Great Pyramids in Egypt. These Stargates are creating energetic portals on the earth plane to help anchor dimensional grids as well as acting as energetic transmitters for the activation of your new crystalline structure. The Stargates are also designed to be a source of light energy during the changing times on your earth plane. With the many physical shifts that will be taking place, these Stargates will provide an energetic balance for you as you go through electrical changes within your system.

The Stargates also provide an energetic portal in which the Star energies can enter the earth plane to assist during this transformational time. The Stargate acts as a doorway for those of us who have pre-agreement connections with the Star energies. It allows you to move through the Stargate for sacred re-connections and communications that are necessary for you to fulfill your own destiny missions.

Going from a third dimensional to a fourth/fifth-dimensional planet creates a huge energetic movement, bringing enormous change within the light frequency of the Earth. There is a tremendous adjustment period required for the completion of these light frequencies to fully anchor and integrate.

With this resurrection of the earth plane, the light frequency on the planet is going to increase and this will create a discrepancy of energies building between dense congested areas on the earth and this light frequency. These pockets of congestion need to be cleared and transformed through some physical shifting and birthing within the earth. With all birthing there is intensity. The Earth needs to come back into a balance. For the balance that is required, there will need to be a repositioning of some land forms throughout the earth plane. This will create a new physical and energetic balance of planet Earth. Each one of you needs to open up to feel the right place for you to be physically on the earth plane. You can trust your placement and know all is in hand for you during this powerful and transformational time as this new quickening of energy is forming on the earth plane. There is a new light essence that is rising on the planet. This light essence is here to support you in your resurrection.

The crop circles are in place to provide important support and stabilization while you are in your birthing process. They are also working in alignment with the Stargates that have reactivated in the great pyramids and the megalith sites to create a series of dimensional grids that enable the Earth to remain in balance through this birthing.

The series of sacred light circles within each crop circle contain the completed blueprint for the Earth changes. These light circles expand the consciousness of the planet and hold the deciphered codes of transformation and understandings for this time. As you are ready, many of you will be given access to these codes. They will be recognized by those of you who are to play a role in creating individual grid lines for specific birthing processes on the earth plane.

Some of you, as part of your mission, have specific work to do in creating energetic vortexes and creating re-alignments through the rivers and mountains. Some of you have a role to play interacting with the crop circles and channeling information from them. Some of you have a role to play in anchoring and holding light frequency holograms that are necessary for the ongoing transformation.

Each one of you is a part of a divine team, and we as a collective are all a part of this Grand Plan. Each one of you is playing your part, whether you are consciously aware of this or not. You are doing what needs to be done. You are working through your guidance, aligning to your soul groups, anchoring vortexes, and working with the power of nature. Know you are doing your work, and playing an essential part in the transformation of your planet. You are making a huge difference!

The Pleiadians provide the tools that will enable you to access information and give you a step-by-step process to initiate these activations. The crop circles hold your awakening codes within your energetic blueprint forms. There is also a series of awakening codes that are being activated through a sound frequency from the crop circles. You can begin to access these high-frequency sounds through your crystalline structure. These sounds are designed to activate and birth energetic alignments through your cells in order for you to continue to integrate to the dimensional energy that is expanding on the planet.

The sound frequency created by the crop circles is responsible for creating a weaving energy in different areas of the earth plane. The weaving is responsible for building new dimensional structures to hold the changing consciousness of our human aspect. This structure is holding a platform for the changing relationship you need to have with your humanness with regard to the ego mind. This is another step toward ending separation inside of your Self.

Remember: This is the time for you to play an active role and consciously choose to move forward, to work with your codes, activating them as they are made available to you. The activation of these codes will link you into new dimensional aspects of Self, and begin to align you more deeply with the energy of your mission. This will allow you to naturally flow and become an even more integral part of the multi-dimensional birthing of this new consciousness as it evolves on the earth plane. You are a gift to the world.

Your cells will go through a transformation with the activation of the codes in your body. You are going to birth a new vibration as you begin to align to the earth's energy through your expanding awareness, as though you will be vibrating in alignment with the earth's energy. This vibrational frequency is your new alignment to doorways into the Universal connection and into the sacred Principles for Living. This vibration holds a frequency of love that carries a new life force. It helps you to align and anchor more easily to the dimensional shifts on the planet. As your vibrational frequency expands you will be able to take a more conscious place within the Collective Consciousness because of your alignment to the Principles for Living.

You have come here to experience re-connection, and the crop circles hold the keys to an awakening of light that has not been available until this time. They are transmitting awakening codes through your crystalline structure. You can open up and consciously begin to interact with the crop circles now. Again, this is about you making a conscious choice to honor your access to your blueprints from the crop circles.

The crop circles are holding individual blueprint energy for every human being on this earth plane. As you move forward into this work the crop circles become more active in their role to assist you in your birthing process. Their energy will help you navigate yourself as the earth changes.

Now let's talk about your blueprint. What is your blueprint? The blueprint, your energetic blueprint, is something that you pre-agreed to make before you came onto this earth plane. At a certain moment before you come onto this earth plane you form a blueprint plan to achieve and complete here within this lifetime. This blueprint holds all the remembering of the completion of your essence and your energy, the full authenticity of your spirit.

The blueprint that you create can be likened to a map. This map contains all that you have chosen for yourself to accomplish in this incarnation, including your mission for this lifetime. It also contains how you choose to live on an energetic level. It influences what direction those choices take you into and which experiences you choose to say yes to experiencing. It also contains all that you want for yourself in your evolution on this earth plane journey.

Once you have fulfilled what is energetically held within your blueprint your life then comes to an end on this earth plane. Understand that you cannot be on this earth plane without an active blueprint. Once your blueprint is fulfilled or completed, you take your next step and leave the planet.

In my first book, I shared my experience of completing my blueprint and creating a new one while I was held by Mother Mary. When you create a blueprint you first lay down the perfection with all aspects of your spiritual soul, of your divine Self. That is the container, and fills the lining of the container. Next, you place within the container all that you wish to fulfill and experience throughout the space of your earth plane journey. Your lining holds the love, truth, and integrity of your spiritual Self and then your journey is placed inside that container so that you are always being held within that space.

Each one of you is always holding yourself with this pure love and pure understanding of your journey. Always. Your blueprint has this as its base for you to access. The time is coming when you will naturally open back to your lining of your container. I am being given a picture of early, early morning when the sun is rising and there is the smallest light on the horizon. Everything else is black. And this light needs to filter slowly through to you, very slowly so that you can receive it. The trickle has already started; that light in the smallest way has already started filtering through to you. This energy is very beautiful and touches my heart. There is tremendous love and this is your love holding you.

At this time the crop circles are ready to release and activate your blueprint energy through you, so you can remember and re-align back to your original light energy. There is a series of energetic sound codes that resonate with their sacred designs.

Your crystalline structure is designed so that the crop circles can work with you electrically through your crystalline structure, transmitting and activating your blueprint codes through you. For the crop circle to transmit the blueprint codes you need to be in your telepathic center to receive them. With that connection established between you and the crop circle, you will begin activating your blueprint codes though the use of the sacred sound. You will then receive the energy of your codes into your body and energetic field. It's through your crystalline structure that you are able to integrate the energy from your blueprint codes and anchor these light forms through your cells.

Your crystalline structure always goes through new levels of activation as you align to the crop circles. These activations create an ongoing regeneration of your cells in your body and your cells begin a self-healing process. This is a natural process. You are re-emerging, moving back to a level of light consciousness through Self. This is part of the grand plan that you have come to fulfill here on the earth plane.

You will then be ready to enter and join the sacred webbing with all the megalith sites and the crop circles on the planet through your telepathic communion abilities. This will birth within you another dimensional level of your connection to the Collective Consciousness. This is a monumental step. You will go through a powerful metamorphosis.

The metamorphosis will get you ready to work with a series of expanded frequencies of light that are going to be anchoring onto your earth plane as you move into the years ahead. These fluid energies of light will create and carry a new level of sound that will be activated and birthed on planet Earth. These sound frequencies will herald in a new time as your crystalline structure is activated on new dimensional levels. For many of you this will create an awakened state of remembering.

Activating Your Sacred Blueprint

Audio file: Chapter 8
Audio file #1

The crop circles work closely with the Pleiadian and Lemurian energies. Here you are going to activate levels of your personal blueprint and activate new levels of your crystalline structure. It is powerful to call on the Pleiadians and the Lemurians to support you in this integration process.

For working with the crop circle you will need:

- Drawing of a crop circle.
- Code Form A.
- Sacred Sound: KEE.

1. Bring the palms of your hands together at the center of your heart line (at the sternum). Bring your Conscious Awareness to where the palms meet and take a Conscious Breath. Let go and move into the alignment, the opening. Feel the opening of your core and allow yourself to anchor, like roots of a tree into the earth.
2. Bring your right hand upward to open into your telepathic center.
3. Expand your telepathic connection by bringing your consciousness into your hand position and letting go. It is through the "letting go" that a deeper alignment can take place within your telepathic center.
4. There is a Code Form A on your crop circle sheet (see Diagram I on the following page). To open into the Code Form you place your Conscious Awareness onto the Code Form A. As you bring your full Conscious Awareness to the Code Form A you will feel it

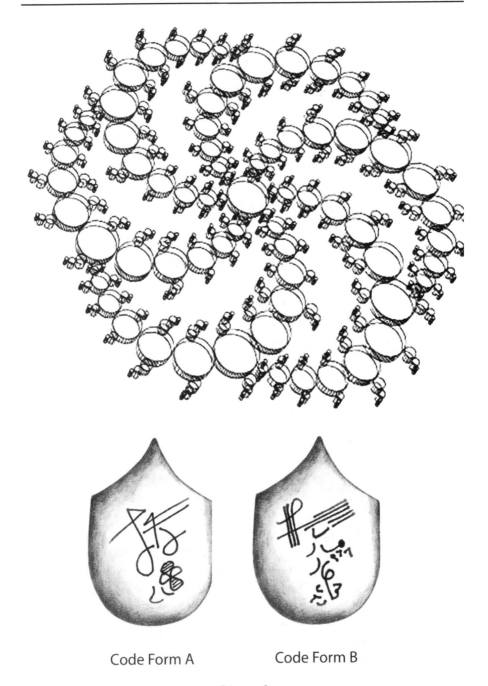

Code Form A   Code Form B

Diagram I

absorbing through your telepathic center. Allow it to fully expand through your telepathic center. Breathe and let go.

5. Bring your Conscious Awareness into the central position of the crop circle. Then place your Code Form A from your telepathic center into the central position of the crop circle. Feel the Code Form being absorbed from your telepathic center into the crop circle. Feel the dimensional doorway open up to you within the crop circle. Just let go and allow yourself to move into the opening. This is a time for you not to do anything, just Be, and allow your full experience of this multi-dimensional light that is birthing you and your crystalline structure.

6. Breathe and feel the lines of energy opening up between you and the crop circle. Feel yourself being received. Open to this communion. Allow your birthing process, however it presents itself.

7. When you feel ready to receive the activation of your personal blueprint:

   A. Place one hand on your heart center and stay within the crop circle energy.

   B. Use the sound KEE. This opens an energetic space within the crop circle and you receive a level of your blueprint energy through a wave of light being released from the crop circle and into you. Here you need to receive the activation through you. Remember: There is an energetic space that opens as you use the sound. You wait for a full opening to take place by seeing, feeling, or sensing the energy of the space, and then let go into that space to become aligned. Only then can you consciously open to receive the blueprint codes. Do not rush your integration.

   C. Use the sound KEE. Each time you use the sound KEE it brings you into another level of access to your blueprint energy. Let go and open to receive. Integrate and let go, allow your birthing process. Remember: There are two birthing processes happening—your crystalline structure is birthing and you are activating your blueprint codes.

   D. When you feel fully aligned with these activations, bring your Conscious Awareness back to your hand position. Wait until you feel all of your awareness coming into the hand. Then come back to your core, with both hands together at the center of your heart line, anchoring through your core. Breathe and keep letting go, allowing all the alignments to integrate through you.

E.　You are going to use a sacred sound through your cells for integration. Allow yourself to become the sound and feel the sound bathe your cells. Let go and Be. This will assist you in integrating your blueprint codes through your cells and energetic field.

Sacred sound: ANAH EE. Continue to use this sound until integration feels complete within you.

Aligning to the Sacred Webbing

Audio file: Chapter 8
Audio file #2

This is a powerful step that you are about to take. Know that you are held and supported as you enter the sacred webbing. Know also that you have a place within the webbing because it aligns and moves through the Collective Consciousness of which you are a part. Once you enter this sacred alliance you will have a more expanded connection to the crop circles, and your telepathic communion center will go through another deeper dimensional expansion.

You will need:

- Your crop circle page.
- Code Form B.
- Sacred sound: ANAH EE.
- Thought code: EE NAE.

1.　Bring the palms of your hands together at the center of your heart line (at the sternum). Bring your Conscious Awareness to where the palms meet, and take a Conscious Breath. Let go and move into the alignment, the opening. Feel the opening of your core, allow yourself to anchor, like roots of a tree into the earth. Use your sacred sound ANAH EE.

　　This will expand your core to another dimensional level, and activate another level of your blueprint codes in readiness to initiate into the webbing. Keep using the sound until you feel the energy is no longer building within your core.

2.　Bring your hand upward to open into your telepathic center.

3. Expand your telepathic connection by bringing your consciousness into your hand position and letting go. It is through the "letting go" that a deeper alignment can take place within your telepathic center. Place the thought code into your telepathic center: EE NAE. This will open up your telepathic center on another level. Bring your Conscious Awareness fully into the space.

4. There is a Code Form B shown on the crop circle sheet in Diagram I on page 102. To open into the Code Form you place your Conscious Awareness onto the Code Form B within the box. As you bring your full Conscious Awareness to the Code Form B, you will feel it absorbing through your telepathic center. Allow it to fully expand through your telepathic center. Breathe and let go.

5. Bring your Conscious Awareness into the central position of the crop circle. Then place your Code Form B from your telepathic center into the central position of the crop circle. Feel the Code Form being absorbed from your telepathic center into the crop circle. Feel the dimensional doorway open up to you within the crop circle. Just let go and allow yourself to move into the opening within the connection to the webbing. Open up your Conscious Awareness through the webbing lines, moving within the flow.

6. Breathe and feel the lines of energy opening up through the webbing lines. Feel your Self being received; open into this communion. Let go and allow the full expansion within this energetic communion, however it presents itself. Now breathe and open into the sound. This is a Universal sound, and as you make it, you are recognized and received here on a different level.

Sacred sound: EE. Expand out the EE and let go. Feel yourself being received more deeply within the telepathic communion of Oneness. Allow your birthing process by letting go. Open into another level of this Universal sound. EE. Expand out the EE and feel it move through you, moving you deeper into this communion experience. Now you are ready to really let go into the sound. EE and just Be.

In this space of being, your energies are being aligned to your place within the webbing. Feel your place and then let go, allowing yourself to anchor within your place. It may feel as though you are traveling through some space; just Be, and allow it. When you are aware that your alignments on this webbing are complete, move your consciousness back to your hand position.

7. Wait until all aspects of your Conscious Awareness are back with your hand. Then move into your core position, with both palms of your hands together at the center of your heart line, anchoring through your core. Breathe and keep letting go, allowing all these alignments to integrate through you. Let them anchor like roots of a tree through you.
8. You are going to use a sacred sound through your cells for integration. Allow yourself to become the sound, and feel the sound bathe your cells. Let go and Be. This will assist you in integrating the energy of place within the sacred webbing. It will expand energy and these new connections through your cells and energetic field.

Sacred sound: ANAH EE. Continue to use this sound until integration feels complete within you. The steps that you take at this moment, as you work with the crop circle and take your place within the sacred webbing, is a life-changing moment. With these powerful and sacred journeys there are new pathways forged within the multi-dimensional aspects of your Self. I know when I entered into these alignments my life changed in so many ways. It was as though I became a part of the sacred energies of the Universe. I felt a new sense of belonging and, most important, inside of me was the sense of returning back to a special place. I was finally able to rest inside myself knowing that a re-connection had been made and there was nothing more to do. I was linked into a flow of connection, a flow of light, and I belonged in this flow. I hold you with love and honor you for all that you are, in this moment.

~~~

Beloved Ones,

We greet you. We call your energies forward to be with us at this pivotal time on your earth plane. We call your hearts forward to play your part now in this highly transformative time. We call you forward to be present in this moment of time with Self, being willing to take a step forward on your path with consciousness and courage.
Be still and know that within this stillness so much can be revealed to you.
Let go and be still. Let us support you within the stillness of your heart.
Take a moment just to Be. Take a step out of your time and join with us in love.

Blessings,
The Pleiadians

~~~

9

The Sacred Matrix

The Pleiadians have been strategically placing the crop circles throughout the earth plane throughout a long period of time. With this New Dawning era, the crop circles have come into their full role. Part of this role involves providing us with the sacred energies of the Matrix. The Matrix is birthed from the multi-dimensional consciousness of the crop circles and is designed to provide access to reawakening codes.

Since the crop circles anchored the sacred webbing around the planet, you are able to work within the sacred Matrix. The sacred webbing is like an energetic womb holding you and supporting you as you move into a birthing process within the Matrix. This process within the Matrix allows you to take steps forward within your awakening process by re-aligning you to the Principles for Living.

The crop circles have created the energetic setting for the Matrix to be able to operate and fully function. The Matrix sources from within the crop circles' multi-dimensional layers, and it holds an energetic consciousness in its own right. The Matrix has been made manifest because of the crop circles' energy and presence on the earth plane.

The Matrix is made up of a series of sacred holographic designs set up to create unique energetic experiences for you. They work in a direct alignment with the crop circles to create an awakening of divine proportions for all human beings. Through these direct experiences, you are able to move into more of an understanding and clarity of your process within your Self.

The holographic designs are sacred in nature and carry a pure essence of light for you to birth through. The holograms were created for your use, but you are only able to utilize them with an authentic quality of love present, which is recognized by your Self. This higher state of Self, this aspect of love that is alive within you, makes it possible for you to receive these series of birthing experiences to take place. Through these experiences of transformation within the Matrix you bring your Self to a place of knowing who you are within the energies of the Collective.

The unique holographic designs within the Matrix create powerful tools for learning, birthing you forward and then connecting you to the energetic makeup within your own multi-dimensional Self. Through a series of learning experiences within the Matrix you gain an understanding of how to work within the energetic process of your multi-dimensionality. Then you begin to integrate these forms of Self. Through this integration process you will begin to consciously utilize these expanded light energies that have anchored within your cells.

The objective of this process is to enable you to anchor the experiences within the cells of your body. The cellular birthing is what allows you to fully utilize your experiences in your life. This is a transformational avenue that will filter slowly through your consciousness, re-activating aspects of your intuition and your higher functioning Self.

The Matrix has been specifically designed for you to have a series of direct sacred experiences for you to know and understand the sacred aspects of your Self within your unlimited experience of Self. You are then able to more fully open into the connection of your place within the collective energies of the Universe by anchoring the energies from the awakening experience through your crystalline structure. These experiences and connections that you form within the Matrix become a permanent natural aspect of your energetic structure. You will be birthing a new dimensional structure within you to house higher energetic levels of your frequency of light. Each journey within the Matrix provides you with a greater sense of Self through these varied journeys and direct experiences.

The Matrix contains elements of what are called "awakening codes" that hold the energy of creation within them. The Matrix has the sole purpose of anchoring dimensional spaces and holding a series of awakening codes in holographic forms. These forms are timeless and limitless, and your job is to activate each series of awakening codes from within the Matrix. You then will journey through the Matrix chambers in order to activate and integrate your awakening codes and, more significantly, open into your true existence energies that are held within the awakening codes.

What I mean by "true existence" is that, within the Matrix chambers, you get to have an experience of many dimensional aspects of your authentic Self.

Through each series of awakening codes you can move into a true form of experience of Self. All your experiences from the Matrix can be energetically held within your crystalline structure for future use. Your crystalline structure has the capacity to hold the many multi-dimensional aspects of you, and also to hold the energetic alignments and forms of your place within the Collective.

There are many multi-dimensional perspectives with which you need to come back into alignment, many aspects of truth of how the Universe truly functions. Within the Matrix journeys you get to experience this from the true perspective rather than from the limited third-dimensional viewpoint of the ego.

There is so much that you do not understand right now within your process, and without that understanding you stay limited. The awakening codes bring you back to a remembering. This will enable you to open up now in your life within this New Dawning and just Be, anchored into your Self as a full memory within the cells. You will be able to flow within the changes with true conscious understanding.

You don't need to necessarily know or understand the whole process before you take this step. You can let go and allow your experience, and you can trust and move forward without hesitation. The gift is here in front of you, and all you need to do is take a jump forward. This is the gift of this sacred time that we have all been given. You are ready for this!

Within this true multi-dimensional world in the Matrix you will be given an internal understanding of your process, which is going to allow you to take your place in your role. Just by accepting this truth, you are moved into your place. After this experience within the Matrix you will effortlessly come back into that full experience of aspects of Self, and just Be; it will be as natural as breathing.

You are ready. As you bring your being forward into your life, all doors open to you. This is because you naturally align through your energetic field. You become a magnet to the experience of Truth. You become your own teacher by bringing the clarity into yourself and then just holding that clarity within you. You become the center of the Universe and all aspects of the Universe by Being. You become Oneness.

Knowledge brings understanding, understanding brings clarity, and clarity brings empowerment.

Don't let your mind get tied up with thoughts about the Matrix. Accept the fact that you will work with the Matrix as a tool to receive these awakening codes. You will move into multi-dimensional direct experiences so that you can receive the divine truths that exist within the dimensional aspects of the Collective Consciousness.

You are going to need some support navigating into some of your experiences. You can give permission for energetic alliances from your pre-agreements to come and assist you in this sacred birthing process.

Now I want to talk about some of the processes you will encounter within the Matrix so you can understand some of the energies you will be accessing. The energies within the Matrix are very different from any you have worked with up to this point. There are no words in our language to accurately describe these multi-dimensional spaces, but I will try to present concepts, which may serve as a base for you to launch yourself into this uncharted territory. Know that these concepts I am presenting may not match your experience because of the multi-dimensional nature of the Matrix and the varied experiences possible.

As you receive your first level of awakening codes you will go through an integration process of fluid energies. Then as the integration of these fluid energies opens through you there will be a series of access doors that begin to open through the Matrix. These doorways will move you into multi-dimensional aspects of alignment to Self and a new state of consciousness. This energy of Being will anchor through the cells of your body and will be recorded by your crystalline structure.

Your divine aspect will move you through the correct doorway for the experience that you are ready to receive. Your job is to just Be and open up your Conscious Awareness into the experience. You may find that you move beyond the need to breathe at this point. There is a dimensional space that does not require any breathing. The energy in this space works directly through your crystalline structure. Your crystalline structure will play an important part assisting you in fully integrating and anchoring these energies as they align energetically with your telepathic center.

Know that within the Matrix your telepathic center will automatically be turned on. You will find yourself placed within energetic communion sessions, which just flow, activating naturally within your telepathic center. These sessions simply manifest a connection through your telepathic center.

You will find yourself operating within very different dimensional experiences as you move into what is called Communion Conferences. These are conducted within a very different setting, with a group of energetic alliances, and there will be sacred forms held within the group for specific initiations for you. These sacred forms are held by your divine element for you and then placed within this Communion Conference for utilization.

These sacred forms activate energetic gifts for you to access at this time on your planet. You will *experience* rather than see, *experience* rather that feel. This is important because it enables you to witness yourself within the experience, without judgment, as you anchor the direct experience within your cells and crystalline structure. This is all created within the dimensional aspects of the Matrix.

During these Communion Conferences you need to let go and open into your telepathic center. Simply allow the full information and teaching to move through you like fluid lines of light text. The text is an energy setting in light that you receive to refer to at another time. It may be that, on another dimensional Matrix journey separate from this one, the text will be utilized.

There will be a series of objectives determined by your divine aspect of Self that will be guiding these Matrix experiences. You need not to worry about how, why, or "Am I doing this right?" The ego mind will have comments to make; however, you need to let go and allow your divine process.

These Communion Conferences and Communion Sessions are created in the moments you are energetically ready for them, when you are ready to receive these specific initiations. You cannot call them forward. They simply appear when you are ready.

I want to remind you that you can call my energy forward at any time for support. I honor you and all that you are as you take these next steps forward toward your Self. Relax and enjoy this aspect of your grand adventure as you are moving into sacred energies of the Matrix. Remember: The Matrix consists of the light consciousness of oneness that you are an aspect! Welcome home!

Activating Your Crystalline Structure in Your Spine

As you work within the Matrix and birth these series of awakening codes, the entire crystalline structure in your body will go through a rapid transformation. Through this rapid transformation of your crystalline structure, from your awakening codes, you are now ready to activate the first level of your crystalline structure in your spine.

The spinal crystalline structure holds a much more expanded frequency of light when activated. The crystalline structure is very different in its form. There is a finer and more expanded aura around the form of crystal. It holds a brilliance within its structure that shoots forth rays of light. The energy of the crystalline structure is like fluid light and these specific activations are regulated through the God Consciousness. This crystalline structure, when activated, links you into the seventh/eighth/ninth-dimensional consciousness. It is potent and powerful. Because of the dynamic energy of the God Consciousness within the spinal crystalline form, the activation is measured in energetic drop forms. You will only activate one drop form at a time within each activation process, so each crystalline activation in the spine is going to activate one drop of "Godhead energy" within you.

The essence of this Godhead energy will bring you into an awakened alignment to a strong loving force within you. Through a mirroring process from the Godhead energy, there is a re-awakening connection of this divine aspect within you. The action of the Godhead drop is birthed through the crystalline activation in the spine.

This activation within your spine will support you by increasing your ability to carry a higher electrical energy within your crystalline structure and cells throughout your body. It will help you navigate more easily through some of the higher dimensional aspects of the Matrix, and it will build all aspects of your crystalline structure to a higher dimensional form through all the cells. This expanded dimensional energetic structure is necessary for you to stabilize during the many energetic processes that you will birth through during the individual journey experiences.

This new dimensional setting within your crystalline structure is going to connect directly through your divine aspect, aligning you to new aspects of being. Understand the "being essence" that is activating is an aspect of your birthright. This birthright energy moves and aligns you automatically beyond the third-dimensional elements and restrictions of the earth plane.

The activation of your crystalline structure within your spine is the next step. You move forward knowing that this activation brings you into direct alignment to the Godhead consciousness. This opens up new avenues for you. This opportunity heralds in your connection to the energies beyond the fifth dimension. Be willing to let go and allow the natural forces on this earth plane to assist you in this integration. Call forth the Lemurian energies, as they specialize in the crystalline adjustments within your body. Open up and call forth these energies to be with you as you take this next step. Lie on the earth. It holds you as your physical cells integrate into the Godhead consciousness energy. Open and receive what is before you with consciousness, love, and courage.

I honor you in this next step.

Spinal Crystalline Structure Activation

Audio File: Chapter 9
Audio file # 1

Find the position on your body first. First feel with your fingers the position of the soft opening on the base of your throat. Just below that soft opening is the bone of the Sternum (see Diagram J). This bone runs down through the center of your chest to just above the solar plexus. You will be working at the very top of the sternum bone, directly below the soft opening in your throat. This position aligns to the crystalline structure within in the spine.

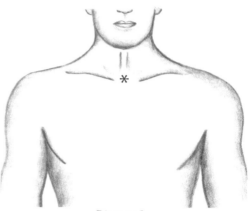

✽ - Position on body, top of sternum

Diagram J

1. Activate your core. This is a very important first step whenever you work within the Matrix. A strong anchoring of the core will support you in moving deeply into all experiences and expanding into different dimensional realms. Bring the palms of your hands together at the center of your heart line (at the sternum). Bring your Conscious Awareness to where the palms meet and take a Conscious Breath. Let go and move into the alignment within your core, the opening. Feel the opening of your core and allow yourself to anchor, like roots of a tree into the earth.

2. Use the two fingers next to your thumb with either your right or left hand. You are going to tap the position with both fingers. Begin above the body and tap on the body once and come up off the body. That's one. Tap again, that's two. Tap again, that's three.

3. Bring both hands outward. Open your hands outward to either side of you, and feel or sense the energy of both hands. Then feel, sense, or see the space created between your hands. Bring your consciousness within the space and breathe and let go. Allow the birthing and expansion to take place within this space.

4. Speak aloud or say to yourself the words: I AM. Feel or sense the energy of the words anchor through you and the space.

    Take your time to fully allow this integration of the energy that anchors from the words. You will say the words I AM a total of three times. Each time you bring the energy of the words through you, integrate the energy that anchors from the words.

5. Come back to your core and fully integrate the birthed energies.

6. You will repeat this full process as described in steps 1, 2, 3, 4, and 5. You will complete three rounds of this process in total. Take the time you need between rounds to fully integrate before starting the next round.

7. When you have completed all three rounds your spinal activation is complete. Lie down. Place your hands on your heart center (this includes the full chest area).

    Bring your full Conscious Awareness to your heart. Bring your breath into the energy of your heart and feel the expansion. Breathe and let go into your heart center. Feel the activation of the energy align through the cells of your body.

Working With the Matrix

Audio file: Chapter 9
Audio file #2

The Matrix has entry points that will assist you now in being able to access your birthing codes for your next transformational step. It has been energetically designed for you, so that you can work within the Matrix and access these multi-dimensional levels for your awakening.

To begin working with the Matrix you need:

- Matrix chart
- Code Form: on Matrix chart. (See Diagram K on page 115.)
- Hand position: full right hand.

1. Activate your core. This is an important first step whenever you work within the Matrix. This anchoring of your core will support you in being able to move deeply into all experiences with the holograms. Bring the palms of your hands together at the center of your heart line (at the sternum). Bring your Conscious Awareness to where the palms meet and take a Conscious Breath. Let go and move into the alignment, the opening. Feel the opening of your core, and allow yourself to anchor, like roots of a tree into the earth. Remember: Allow full expansion of your core before moving on.

2. Place your right palm over the Matrix chart and feel the energetic connection building between you as you bring your conscious awareness into the Matrix. Let go and allow the energy to build between you and the Matrix chart. Let go and breathe and experience how the connection between you and the Matrix chart

Diagram K

births. Note: Your telepathic center automatically begins to open as you align with the Matrix energy. The Matrix can identify and recognize your unique energetic frequency through your palm. Your right palm holds a blueprint of your unique frequency signature of your divine element. Let go into the deepening connection with the consciousness of the Matrix.

3. You are going to use the Code Form on your Matrix page. The Code Form is in the triangular box (this will open up a doorway for you to gain access as an entry point into your Matrix).

    Bring your consciousness into the Code Form. Just allow this Code Form to be absorbed-by your telepathic center. You do this by simply placing your consciousness onto the Code Form within the triangle. You will begin to feel or sense it slowly being absorbed by your telepathic center.

4. Place the Code Form from your telepathic center into the Matrix. Do this by bringing your consciousness into the Matrix, and you will feel or sense the Code Form being absorbed by the Matrix. Open to the Matrix and feel a deepening of connection between you, as there is a forging of energy between you.

5. Now you are going to begin your journey into the Matrix. You need to first choose your dimensional entry position for this journey: #1, #2, #3, or #4. You have four possible choices, knowing that each journey you take can be in a different entry position or the same as before. Each entry position holds multi-dimensional experiences within them, so you need to tune to what feels right for you in this moment. Place your index finger on the entry position you have chosen within your Matrix chart. Bring your consciousness to the chosen entry position doorway. This is where your index finger is touching. Connect to the energy within the doorway. Now use the thought code AE SHEE. Remember: You are going to place the thought code into the doorway.

    The doorway will open. Allow your conscious awareness to be moved within the Matrix flow. Let go into the flow and be with your experience as you expand through the space.

6. When you feel you have fully moved within your experience, send the thought code AE SHEE. Place the thought code wherever you are in the flow of the Matrix. Then open up to the first series of your awakening codes. The awakening codes will move you within the chambers of the Matrix. Allow your experience and open into what the chambers are presenting to you.

7. Now that you are in the chamber it is time for you to consciously activate your experiences from the awakening codes you have received. Do this by letting go and opening up through your telepathic center. Make a statement of readiness for your experience with the activation of these first series of awakening codes you have received. For example: I am ready now for the activation of my awakening codes to begin.

8. When your experience feels complete, slowly place your index finger back on the doorway that you entered. Bring your full Conscious Awareness to that place, making sure that all parts of you are at that point. Take all the time you need to feel yourself fully come back to that point. Breathe and let go and allow the energetic alignments through your cells.

9. Come back into your core with the palms of your hands together. Anchor this energy through your core allowing the core expansion, like roots of a tree going down into the earth. Then integrate outside with the natural forces. Sit or lie on the earth and breathe.

   Don't forget to rest after the activations. It will support you and the cells of your body to fully open and receive. Don't let your mind start dissecting your experience. Just breathe and let go. I honor you for taking this step.

~~~

Beloved Ones,

With the new energies anchoring onto your planet we call to you to begin to allow your Self to harness these light force energies through you. It is again about Conscious Choice, opening up to receive this pure light force that can move through your crystalline structures within your body.

This gift of light is yours. It has your unique signature of essence within it. As you consciously receive it within your energetic field, your crystalline structure can birth to another level. This is your conscious choice in action.

Take your Conscious Breath and open up to drink it into your cells. Bring your Conscious Awareness forward and breathe into your cells, receiving the light frequency. This is all about you being willing to receive what is yours.

We witness you as you birth, as you receive. This is your creation; utilize it!

Blessings,
The Pleiadians

~~~

10

Activating Your Command Energy: Conscious Choice to Activate Your Energetic Portals

Your Command Energy is a process of re-birthing your Self through the Conscious Choice action of invocation. Invocation is the action of "calling forth," awakening your Command Energy through the use of a sacred sound. This is a powerful Conscious Choice action. By awakening your Command Energy you are saying yes to an aspect of your personal power by creating a new alignment to your divine aspect and anchoring this aspect within the cellular structure of your cells. This action accumulates permanent alignments to Self that you will be able to draw upon as you have a need. You will find that your energetic connections to other life force groups, your channel, and your ability to perceive truth, expand naturally as you anchor through your Command Energy to your Self. Now is the time to consciously align to what the Pleiadians call your Command Energy.

Your Command Energy is anchored through an energetic portal within your heart center. Birthing your energetic portal will activate a beautiful and profound process within you. This connection to your portal will allow you to begin a new journey of communion with the higher light aspects within the Collective Consciousness of the Universe and enable you to hold your place within a higher-dimensional frequency of love. Know that you will be held as you birth, and witnessed as you say yes to another step in your journey.

The energetic portal that is going to birth through your heart center will open up to become a multi-dimensional receiving station. The Pleiadians often refer to this portal as your "sacred heart receiver." This energetic portal carries multi-dimensional aspects of love, and this opening will enhance your ability to receive divine aspects of Self that hold a higher frequency of love than you have previously aligned to before in this lifetime. There will be ongoing opportunities to birth into dimensional extensions within this portal.

As your portal is birthed, your crystalline structure within your heart center will also begin a transformation. The crystalline structure will become pure and clear as the frequency within the crystalline form begins to expand, allowing the crystalline form to birth into a much higher frequency of light. Your crystalline structure begins to *hum* with this new vibration. This *hum* is an awakener. The action created from the hum begins to open up an energetic womb, activating a birthing process that expands out through your energetic field in readiness for you to anchor your Command Energy. Your energetic field is going to work in alignment with the portal opening within your heart, carrying the essence from the activation of your Command Energy. Your right of Conscious Choice to activate the crystalline structure within your heart has made it possible for you to anchor the high frequency of light that will birth from you, activating your Command energy.

As you invoke the sacred sound you need to open up and feel the power of your invocation, and open to the essence of your energy as it opens up through you. You will be able to feel and experience the creation of your Command Energy build from the use of your unique frequency of the sound as you bring it forth. As you invoke your Command Energy you will be able to experience a new sense of power and strength within you.

I know that as I began to invoke my Command Energy for the first time I had a profound experience. As I expanded, using my Command Energy, there was a sense of a building strength through me on a physically level. Energetically, I could feel levels of life force building within me. Connecting to this aspect of my power was an exhilarating and exciting experience. As I invoked the Sacred Sound, I found that I became part of the sound, and after a while I did not even recognize my own voice. The sound and quality that was emerging from me was unfamiliar, and at the same time it was very compelling to continue to unfold into this amazing essence. I felt a deep peace and contentment moving through me as my Command Energy continued to anchor.

I found it was important to make the sacred sound and then give myself a moment to experience my energy that was flowing through me, and then to bring another sound forward and focus on being that sound. The more I worked with the sound the more stable I became within the experience of my Self that I was reunited with through my Command Energy.

Now your next step is to invoke your Command Energy through the sacred sound. When you use this sacred sound you begin a process of building your Command Energy through your cells and through your core. This life force energy holds your divine signature of the Oneness, so as it anchors a natural part of you, there is a continual building of this sacred alignment to your Self.

Remember: As you use the sacred sound there is an anchoring of your Command Energy opened through your sacred heart space into your portal. Your heart cells recognize the essence of your Command Energy and begin to expand. The picture that comes to mind is of a sun rising through each cell and each cell sending shafts of light outward into your energetic field.

Your Command Energy is actually your own *life force* light. You are not working with anyone else's light. So once more, you are birthing you in this process. This aspect of your Command Energy is coming from your own divine source. As you evoke this re-connection you become the sound. This process is more than alignment; there is a permanent connection established. You open up a dimensional bridge that stays aligned, so you are in a state of a permanent re-union with your Command Energy. This bridge is anchored through to the portal within your heart.

Your Command Energy births in increments so that you can fully integrate the changing levels of electrical light anchoring through you. Your crystalline structure is designed to support the integration of this new electrical component of your energy.

Through your Command Energy you are working from a higher-frequency level of Self so you will be able to perceive energies from these higher dimensional states. This gives you a "bird's eye view," beyond the third-dimensional illusion and drama of the earth plane, and allows you to participate more fully within the Universal realms.

When you activate your Command Energy you will experience a natural magnification of all your energetic experiences on the earth plane as well as within the Universe. You have an expanded ability to perceive energies and to experience truth. You will find your abilities to connect and work with people greatly enhanced.

You will also experience expanded relationships with energetic alliances, because you will be able to meet these energies from a much more stable energetic place within your Self. Your light energy will allow natural alignments to bring you clearer connection and communication.

After a time, you will no longer need to evoke your Command Energy to experience your alignment; it will become a natural part of you. You simply will Be in your Command Energy. As you unfold you will carry more expanded aspects of your Command Energy and you will find that there will be a continual expansion of connection to your Command Energy as a natural part of your awakening process.

You will be given steps and tools to activate your Command Energy and then ways to access your natural alignment to this aspect of Self. This is always done through your heart center. You evoke your Command Energy and then anchor your Command Energy within the stable access point of your energetic portal in your heart center.

Evoking your Command Energy with the sacred sound is a powerful and empowering experience. It is joyful because you are accessing your Command Energy through conscious action: reclaiming your power. You feel connection to your source, a sense of peace, of remembering, and often of liberation.

You may feel something being unleashed, set free. The burdens from lifetimes of third-dimensional experiences simply drop away as you take back your power. Once you anchor your Command Energy, your third-dimensional burdens can no longer be held within your body.

As you begin to birth your Command Energy, your energetic field begins to reflect your birthed light energy. It comes in the form of a pulsating light frequency out into the Universe, allowing your energetic aspect to return to your place within the Universal Grid. Your sacred place expands within the Grid as an aspect of you comes home in that moment. Your complete dimensional perspective is altered, which allows you to fully participate within the Universe, taking your place through all realms. This is part of the sacred design that has been set down for this New Dawning time for each one of you.

Your Command Energy allows a natural healing energetic process to begin working within your physical body. You will have access to work with your natural life force healing energy, your expanded gifts, and to experience an aspect of Oneness, of Universal connection. The more you choose to utilize this aspect of Self, the more your cells carry an expanded essence of your Command Energy.

By invoking your Command Energy you begin to align to an expanded aspect of your Life Force Breath, which is birthed through your lungs. You may find that you become more aware of your breath and the role that it plays as you work with your Command Energy. You are already familiar with what the Pleiadians call the Conscious Breath and how important it is within your birthing and integration experiences. This life force breath is an expanded aspect of this breath, and it is going to impact and enhance your experiences, because you will be bringing forth a breath that carries your Command Energy. This life force breath is actually the "Conscious Breath" with Conscious Awareness and intention focused as the breath is placed into the desired place. Your breath carries a "light force" of your divine aspect. You will find that, as you use this Life Force Breath, an energetic quickening and expansion of light will assist in birthing what it is that you desire. Bringing the life force energy into your creation will assist in manifesting your goals. Similarly, you can bring the Life Force Breath into your Self to accelerate a healing process.

Know that all aspects of creation require the life force breath. This needs to be used through Conscious Choice action, opening up in a moment and bringing awareness with your life force breath as you work. Bring your expanded breath into your creations, and feel or sense the action of this breath. Experiment and witness yourself within the "life force" action of the breath. Feel *you*. Sense yourself within the energy of this breath. The more you work consciously with this expanded breath, the more quickly your Life Force Breath will be able to birth to new expanded levels.

The cells of your lungs will go through a metamorphosis as they expand with the frequency of your Life Force Breath. This light force energy will move from your lungs to enter all of your cells, strengthening the cells, and rejuvenating all the cells within your body. Every cell in your body will be impacted by this new light frequency that is activated through your Life Force Breath.

As you work through these different levels your sacred heart center will dimensionally expand because of the new energy carried within every cell from your Life Force Breath.

A part of your crystalline structures role is to transmit your Command Energy outward, making it possible for you to align into this transmitting energy force of your Self. You always need to have a reason to activate your Command Energy. You channel that desire as you move into the action of evoking your Command Energy.

The new dimensional energies on the planet are creating a transformation with the natural forces as the veils continue to lift. The further expansion of your crystalline structure through the re-birthing of your Command Energy is going to allow you to consciously harness the natural forces energy to assist you in your integration of your Command Energy through your cells. This is a part of the natural forces new role in the New Dawning time, which supports us in the integration of these newly birthed energies.

Now is the time to prepare this portal within your heart center so that you can create a place to anchor your Command Energy. You will be working on expanding the energetic level of your heart center by using a sacred sound. The cells in your heart will respond to your unique frequency of sound, and the anchoring portal will be birthed. The crystalline structure within your heart will simultaneously be activated to a higher frequency by the anchoring of this portal.

Expanding the Crystalline Structure of Your Heart to Birth Your Portal

Audio file: Chapter 10
Audio file #1
Sacred sound: KEE NAH SAE
Sacred sound: EE

1. Bring the palms of your hands to your full heart center (this is the full chest area). Bring your Conscious Awareness to the pressure of your hands, the warmth of your hands, and take a Conscious Breath. Bring your Conscious Awareness deeper into your heart center. Allow yourself to let go, deeper into the energetic opening within your heart center.

2. Now bring your Conscious Awareness deeper into an opening. You are going to birth your heart center energetically with a sacred sound in order to prepare the heart for the birth of the portal. Use the sacred sound: KEE NAH SAE. Bring the sound into the cells of your heart, then bring your Conscious Awareness into the cells and breathe. Let go. Feed this sound into the cells of your heart until there is an expansion of light. You may see, feel, or sense this; it may present as heat, vibration, or color within the cells. Allow your experience.

3. Bring your Conscious Awareness into the light that is birthing within the cells. Feel how the light is expanding and beginning to birth the form of the portal. Use the sacred sound: EE. You bring this sound right into the form of the portal, and feel how it begins to transform and anchor. Keep using the sound EE until the portal has fully expanded. You may see, feel, or sense this. Let go and allow your experience.

4. Now bring your Conscious Awareness out into your energetic field by moving your Awareness beyond your physical form. Open to the energetic flow and the patterns of energy. Touch them with your Conscious Awareness and bring your Conscious Breath into them. Let go. Open the palms of your hands to receive this flow and these patterns. As you bring your Conscious Awareness to your palms, the flow and the patterns move into your hands.

5. Now bring the palms of your hands back onto your heart center. Feel the flow and the patterns move into your heart center, into the portal. Bring your Conscious Awareness back to the portal. Use the sound EE into the portal. Feel the birthing of this flow move into the portal, birthing a dimensional energy through the portal. Use the sound EE until the portal is completely anchored and expanded dimensionally.

6. Bring your full consciousness back into your heart center, opening into your hands with your consciousness and bringing a focus of your energy into the cells of the heart. Breathe and integrate this energy through you and all your cells. Don't rush this process. Then you need to go on to the earth and integrate this transformational energy from the anchoring of your portal.

Activating Your Command Energy

Audio file: Chapter 10
Audio #2
Command energy activation sacred sound: ASHA TAE
Sacred sound: EE

Now that you have activated your energetic Portal in your heart center you are ready to be able to activate your Command Energy and have it anchor within the energetic portal.

1. Bring the palms of your hands to your full heart center (this is the full chest area). Bring your Conscious Awareness to the pressure of your hands, the warmth of your hands, and take a Conscious Breath. Bring your Conscious Awareness deeper into your heart center. Allow yourself to let go, deeper into the energetic opening within your heart center.

2. Let yourself align to your energetic portal by simply bringing your Conscious Awareness toward the portal and use the sacred sound EE. This will align you energetically to your portal. Use your Conscious Breath. This will bring you deeper into this alignment with the portal.

3. Now you are going to activate your Command Energy using the sacred sound ASHA TAE. As you use the sound, feel the presence of energy build within you as you make the sound. Connect with it consciously as you make the sound. Feel the sound resonate within you. Keep connecting to the sound and wait for the building and anchoring of your Command Energy through you.

4. Bring your Conscious Awareness into the portal. Bring your Command Energy sound into the portal: ASHA TAE. Feel your Command Energy anchoring through the portal, and then experience the transformation of the portal's energy as the anchoring takes place. Let go into the expanding energy.

5. Bring your Conscious Awareness to your heart center. Feel the expansion of light that has been activated through the cells of your heart. Your crystalline energy within your heart is beginning to transform with the activation of your Command Energy. Use your Conscious Breath and feel. Experience how your life force energy breath may have changed. Allow your full experience. Know that your Command Energy activations are cumulative, so each time you activate your Command Energy your alignments will become stronger.

Creating Your Circle of Light

Audio file: Chapter 10
Audio file #3
Command energy activation sacred sound: ASHA TAE
Sacred sound: EE

Through the activation of your Command Energy you are now able to create a circle of light using your Command Energy. Within this circle of light you can work on your own self-healing through a rejuvenation of your cells and receive knowledge and clarity from the higher-dimensional realms. Each time you create a circle of light you are able to anchor and integrate expanded levels of your Command Energy.

Before you begin, six clear quartz crystals need to be programmed (see Diagram L). The crystals need to be very small. To program the crystals, place your six crystals on the Programming Map (see Diagram L) for two days before using them to activate your circle of light.

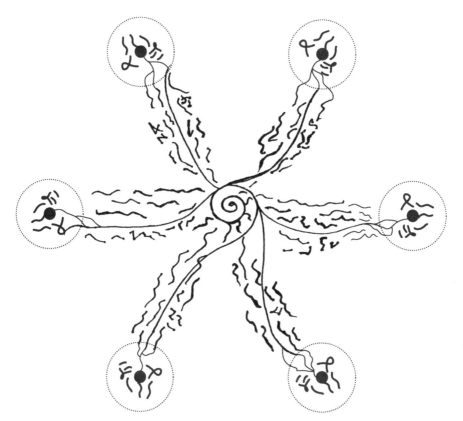

Diagram L

Get your crystals ready to do your work by placing all six crystals to form a circle. Your crystals must be evenly spaced. Your circle can be large or small, but it does need to be big enough for you to sit in (on the ground or in a chair), and stand or lie down. When you are working in your circle you need to be in the central position, so make enough room for your place. You may find that you will need to lie down and integrate within your circle after you have completed your work.

To create your circle, lay out your six crystals. One crystal is directly in front of you. One crystal needs to be directly behind you. The other crystals are then placed with two on either side and evenly spaced to create your circle. Be aware that you need a proper circle, so take your time to place the crystals correctly. It does not have to be perfect, but it does need to hold an energy form so that you can do your work and create the correct energy. The Circle Layout-Placement of Crystals can be found in Diagram M.

Inside your circle, take water to drink and something to sit on. This can be a cushion, chair, or anything else. You may also want to take a pad and pen. Now you are ready to begin your work process and activating your Circle of Light. To begin this process you should be sitting in the central position within your circle.

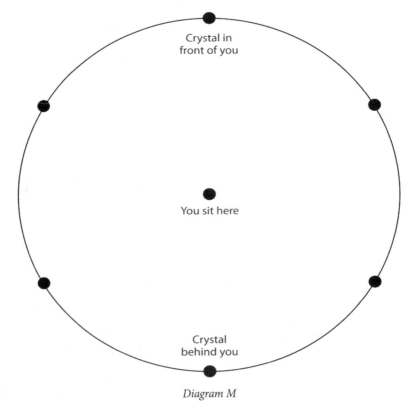

Diagram M

1. Bring the palms of your hands to your full heart center (this is the full chest area). Bring your Conscious Awareness to the pressure of your hands, the warmth of your hands, and take a Conscious Breath. Bring your Conscious Awareness deeper into your heart center. Allow yourself to let go, deeper into the energetic opening within your heart center.

2. Let yourself align to your energetic portal by simply bringing your Conscious Awareness toward the portal and use the sacred sound EE. This will align you energetically to your portal. Use your Conscious Breath. This will bring you deeper into this alignment with the portal.

3. Now you are going to activate your Command Energy using the sacred sound ASHA TAE. As you use the sound, feel the presence of energy build within you as you make the sound and connect with it consciously as you make the sound. Feel the sound resonate within you. Keep connecting to the sound and wait for the building and anchoring of your Command Energy through you.

4. Bring your Conscious Awareness outward to all six crystals that make up your circle. Open up your Conscious Awareness and your Command Energy begins to build a connection to all six crystals. Then activate your Command Energy using the sound ASHA TAE. As you do this all six crystals begin to connect as your Command Energy builds. You create this full circle of light through your Command Energy.

5. Let go into your circle of light with your Conscious Awareness. Allow yourself to unfold and birth with this circle of light. Use your life force energy and breathe to expand your creation of your circle of light.

6. When you are ready you can expand the dimensional energy within your circle of light and bring your Conscious Awareness into the portal. Use the sacred sound EE into the portal and then feel a deeper anchoring of your Command Energy within your portal.

7. Now transmit your Command Energy sound ASHA TAE. Using your hands you are going to work with your Command Energy to expand out your circle's energy. Work with your hands to move your Command Energy into the existing circle boundary toward the crystals. Use your expanding creative breath to allow this birthing expansion of your circle of light.

8. Let go into this expanded energy within your circle of light, bringing your Conscious Awareness into your full circle energy. Let go and just Be.

9. There is a webbing that begins to form within your circle. Become a part of this divine dimensional web that you are birthing through your circle of light. Let go and allow your experience. Use your expanded breath and Conscious Awareness to move into this dimensional webbing. Next, bring your Command Energy sound ASHA TAE into the webbing so that you can begin to align to the webbing for healing and a regeneration of your cells.

Let go and allow this birthing to take place through you. Take all the time you need to fully align and integrate this energy. You may feel a need to lie down and rest within your circle of light. It is important not to rush this process. Let go and allow your full experience. Remember: It is through letting go that you allow the full alignments.

As I began to create my first circle of light I was filled with the powerful experience that I was the creator of this circle. As I opened to that truth there was an anchoring of light that birthed through me, and I was transformed as I claimed this truth. Know that you hold the keys to your own awakening. Don't hold back these truths. Own who you are in these turning-point moments of your ability to create with your Command Energy. As your Command Energy develops you align on another level to the Principles for Living, taking another step toward home.

You can work within your circle of light to create what it is you need for yourself at this time. You can work on physical areas of your body that require healing. The cells of your body will begin a regenerative process within your circle of light, or you can simply rest in the light within your circle and Be.

~~~

Beloved Ones,

We greet you. We hold the energetic space for each one of you to understand the role you play right now in your life, a powerful role that gives you access to your own divine Command Energy. Know that you hold the power to transform your Self; you hold the power to self-heal.

There is Command Energy within you that you can access, and it involves simply knowing that you have the right to open up into your Command Energy with a Conscious Breath, calling forward your essence. Not through ego will but through your sacred heart connection. Simply opening up through your heart and calling forth your own healing energy.

Your energy is now available for use and as you step forward and anchor this command essence you begin a new birthing process within your cells. Your divine signature begins to activate through your crystalline structure, and your crystalline structure begins to light up with your sacred essence.

Be here now with your Command Energy. Be here now with your conscious commitment to your Self. Take your place now in this moment and feel your energy begin to build through you with each conscious committed breath.

We witness you.
The Pleiadians

~~~

11

Working With Your Command Energy and the Earth's Natural Energies: Creating Energetic Alliances

The activation of your Command Energy has begun, and a stable alignment through your portal within your heart center now exists for you. You also have a direct opening into the many multi-dimensional levels to the Principles for Living. This is going to support you in moving rapidly into expanded connections within the consciousness of the Collective Energies, bringing you into alignments that you have not experienced at this point in time. Changes within your DNA strands can take place because you have taken this powerful Conscious Choice connection to your Command Energy. Birthing the portal within your heart allows you to process the elements of Being that are contained within the Principles for Living. These sacred elements are then able to align through your cells and create a re-positioning of your DNA strands, sparking an evolution within you.

Because of this huge energetic shift, now it is time to expand to other dimensional settings using your Command Energy consciously in your life. This involves working with a series of specific processes that will anchor an alignment through you, so you will no longer need to activate your Command Energy consciously; there will be a completed union process activated so that you will simply Be your Command Energy. It will become a natural aspect of you.

As you begin this next level of your work, you will come to another turning point in your awakening process. You take another step because you are consciously participating within the Universe on a higher level. More important, you are consciously channeling and utilizing your divine aspect as a human being. You are waking up as you align through a higher dimensional state of Self. You begin to fully participate through the expanded dimensional alignments within the Universe when you consciously open to work through your Command Energy. When you begin to access these expanded dimensional alignments within the Universe you activate what is called your "Destiny line."

Your Destiny line is an active bridge that directly connects to your blueprint and unlocks the option to change your blueprint. However, it only opens up for this blueprint change if you have an unexpected acceleration in your awakening process. For example, making the Conscious Choice to activate your Command Energy and move into the alignments of the Principles for Living creates the need to adjust your blueprint energy so that you can move on your advanced pathway of awakening.

You do not need to be aware of the details of these new activations within your blueprint. Your divine aspect through your Command Energy will create a series of new energetic signatures that are required for these new activations and adjustments within your blueprint.

This is an exceptional time for all of you who are awake. Each one of you is given a grace right now. This is like no other time in this planet's history. Everything is in place for you to open to these many opportunities, to quickly move forward. The doors are opening wide as you activate your Command Energy and step forward, moving on your Destiny line, birthing another level of the energy of your blueprint, and working within your sacred trust.

Sacred Trust

This pathway within your Destiny line can recalibrate the energetic configuration within your energetic field, which moves you into an expanded enlightenment flow. This enlightenment flow in turn brings you into the sacred trust that you created for yourself to receive, if and when you came to this juncture on your journey.

You set up your own sacred trust before you came to this earth plane. Your sacred trust holds tools and teachings that *you* put in place to utilize now. You only receive within your sacred trust what you are energetically ready for, reuniting with sacred tools that belong to you. You can't choose what it is you want to receive because this has been a pre-destined choice that you made for yourself.

The sacred trust energies are designed to take you to another level, to bring you to another viewpoint within the Collective Consciousness energy of which you are a part. Up to this point, you have not been ready to fully align or be given access to many dimensional aspects within the Collective Conscious.

Through the anchoring of your Command Energy you can now move into these expanded alignments within the Collective Consciousness and have access to your sacred trust. This will bring you into a powerful state of Being. The tools and teachings from your sacred trust will help you integrate and become part of these higher levels. This is why your sacred trust is being made available to you now.

The Pleiadians are holding energetic platforms open for you to unlock your bridge, accessing your Destiny line. They are also setting energetic containers in place for you to access the energy of your current blueprint and to activate the new imprinting energies of your blueprint. You are ready for a new level of your mission.

You will be given a step-by-step process to access your sacred trust and receive the tools and teachings. The previously placed tools that were meant to be received now come in many different forms, such as energy coming into you, geometrical forms, and physical power objects such as swords and crystals. You may be offered a chalice, you may feel heat moving through you, or you may feel a form of love coming into you. These are just some examples of what you may receive in your sacred trust.

By placing your Conscious Awareness and Life Force Breath into what you have received from your sacred trust, you activate and are given access. The energy will begin to transform, for example, transmitting knowledge and teachings or high frequencies of light into you. This is what can take place when you bring your consciousness into the experience, the object, the energy, or the sensation.

Everything you receive within your sacred trust holds awakenings for you. You receive a gift, but that gift needs to be opened, unwrapped by your Conscious Awareness with your Conscious Life Force Breath. Receive the gift and don't leave it unwrapped. Open and explore what you have been given! Activate one process within your sacred trust at a time, remembering that you have left this gift for your Self to be utilized at this time. It is essential to then fully integrate each process you have received.

When I first received from my sacred trust I was given a circle, and I thought, "What can I do with a circle?" I wanted something magical like a crystal or a wand! Of course my ego mind wanted those things. I was reminded by the Pleiadians that I had placed this circle for me to receive now and I needed to explore this gift. So I brought my Conscious Awareness to the circle and took a breath; as I did, this the circle began to light up and expand. I opened up and received the light through my cells. I then brought my Conscious Awareness deeper and placed a Life Force Breath into the light. As I did this, I received powerful love and knowledge as I was taken into the circle and held. So it is important to open into the many levels of the gift within your sacred trust. Keep opening up the gift by touching it with your Conscious Awareness and letting go.

As you access the expanded experiences through your sacred trust you are returned to more aspects of Self, and this allows you to begin a sacred alliance with the natural forces. This alliance is part of your mission in this lifetime. It's an aspect of returning to Oneness with all life force.

The Natural Forces

The natural forces on the earth plane are going through a rapid transformation on many dimensional levels. The veils have lifted in order for you to work with these energies of nature through your Command Energy. Working with the natural forces is going to allow you to end a level of separation within you, because you will move into a new aspect of the Oneness through this sacred communion. This will allow you to open into a state of Oneness and expand your heart center through these alliances. You have a tremendous opportunity to harness the energies of the natural forces through you, so that you can continue to integrate each dimensional shift as it takes place on the earth plane. You will be able to hold a platform of support for the earth changes as the dimensional shifts take place.

You will receive a series of sacred alignments through your crystalline structure for your integration on a cellular level. Working with a sacred communion and alliance, through the utilization of your Command Energy, you can begin journeying into an experience of Oneness with the collective natural force energies.

It is possible for a sacred union to form between your essence within your Command Energy and the natural forces. This is a truth. Part of your destiny is moving into an alignment of a sacred communion with the natural forces. As you open into this union your Command Energy can expand and your portal within your heart center can transform dimensionally to hold this communion connection. Your heart will birth dimensionally as a natural receiving station when working with the natural forces. These initiating elements held within the natural forces enable your heart to unfold through these new multi-dimensional alignments within the portal of your heart. The natural forces contain powerful elements of the Principles for Living. As you are naturally realigned you begin to free flow with new sacred truths.

When you work with the natural forces through your Command Energy you always work through your telepathic center. You begin by working through a telepathic communion connection to align within the sacred connections of light that are held within the Oneness of nature. This energy of Oneness births through you for your transformation.

When you make a telepathic communion connection it is helpful to begin with a form in nature that is stable; for example, a mountain, tree, flower, or rock. You must choose what you are going to connect with first and then begin the process of telepathic alignment with your Command Energy.

Be aware that you may have in your mind what you will connect to, however, at the moment of connection you can be moved to connect to something else in nature. Realize that most likely your original idea was from the ego mind, and you are being moved by your divine aspect to a supportive connection for you in this moment. *You can trust your experience.*

When you do connect through your Command Energy with any aspect of nature, you may find that your experience of the form within the connection is presenting differently in its energetic state. Remember: You are working through your Command Energy, which is beyond third dimension. You are aligning on a fourth/fifth- and possibly sixth-dimensional experience to that nature form. You are experiencing the multi-dimensional energetic aspect of this nature form within your telepathic communion connection. So the energy of the form in nature that you are connecting might seem incredibly large or changed in shape because you are viewing the full energetic essence of the nature form. Be aware the forms in nature, the form of you, are different when experienced outside the third-dimensional aspect. The telepathic experience takes you beyond the third-dimensional setting.

Working through the world of the natural forces can be disorientating and confusing as you begin aligning within this multi-dimensional space. It moves to a different rhythm than the energetic world of the spiritual realms. The energies of the natural forces have a collective energetic formation to them, which will bring you into unique experiences. They are part of the Oneness, but they operate from an energetic setting that many of you have not experienced before in this lifetime. Do not doubt your place within these interactions. You do have a place within this setting; it's just different. It's important to embrace an aspect of you that belongs here—that has always belonged here.

When you work with the natural forces a powerful interaction takes place between you and whatever form of nature you choose to align with. This interaction is going to stretch your capacity by expanding your energies out to new levels. This may be daunting at first, but it is the time for you to grow and allow this next step of sacred communion and re-union with these aspects of the natural forces.

Use the earth's energy to support you by anchoring strongly into the earth before you begin your alignments. You can do this by physically sitting on the earth. Feel yourself being taken into the earth. Or you may feel a physical connection through the soles of your feet as you stand on the earth. When you complete your telepathic process it's also very important to use the earth as an integration tool. Lie on the earth and let go. Allow yourself to integrate through the earth's energy. Feel the earth beneath you, holding you. Breathe your Life Force Energy.

Working with your Command Energy, with this telepathic communication and the natural forces, you can greatly assist with the transition of the planet. For many of you, part of your mission is to work in setting up new energetic grid lines to assist in the birthing of this new dimensional energy anchoring on to the earth plane now. Many of you have other roles to play with the natural forces on the planet. These roles will be revealed to you as you journey through this sacred communion with your Command Energy.

In turn, the natural forces play a powerful part in the integration of your crystalline structure and greatly support you in your awakening process. As you connect to the natural forces there is a strong healing energy that comes into the cells of your body through this sacred communion. You become re-aligned within your body systems through the pure essence of nature, which rebalances the body and feeds the spirit of your nature, bringing peace and a deep stillness within.

In this New Dawning you are destined to come into this alignment with nature and you are meant to work together in a Conscious Choice alliance. This pre-agreement step moves you toward that natural alliance and brings you one step closer to achieving enlightenment.

My awakening with the natural forces was a profound and essential aspect to my physical and emotional healing. Through nature I was able to first connect to my inner kids. It was a safe place for me to meet the very sad and hurt aspects of myself. Many times I was held by the elements of the Earth Mother, held by the energy of Father Sun. Being held by these powerful forces supported a re-balancing of my emotional aspect. My first experience with nature came as I left my first sweat lodge.

I entered the sweat lodge with no connection to any aspect of nature or the natural forces. During the journey I came face to face with a mountain of fear. The only way I could survive the overwhelming fear was to place my little finger in the earth, and I experienced being held by Mother Earth. I placed all of my focus on this connection.

It was through the miraculous power of this connection that I was able to stay with my journey and complete the sweat. I came out of the sweat lodge renewed and had the direct experience that my fears could never hurt me. As I looked around me I heard the rocks talking to me, and I could feel the essence of the trees and the earth. From that time, my re-connection to the natural forces continued to expand and I regained a trust of life.

As I moved forward with my personal healing I began a deep initiation through the shamanic worlds with the Pleiadians, and began to harness this connection on a conscious level. Through a powerful re-awakening of my shaman aspect I formed a natural re-alliance with all aspects of the shamanic worlds. This was a liberating but challenging experience for me, as I came back into a place of Oneness with nature, taking back my full place of power with the Elders of the Sacred Lodge.

Enlightenment comes through the ending of separation, through reunion with your divine aspect, and with all life force in the Universe. As you work in a sacred telepathic communion with the natural forces you end another aspect of separation within you. This is part of the destiny of all human beings in this lifetime!

Creating Your Own Energetic Alignments

Now is the time to create your own energetic alignments so that you can birth and anchor your "sacred signature" through your energetic field. Your sacred signature contains a unique aspect of your divine light, which interacts through the Universe, opening up dimensional spaces that connect you into the Principles for Living. I liken it to a fingerprint. You are recognized and honored for the sacred essence that you carry within your unique signature, and you are automatically linked into these sacred principles for your continuing resurrection process.

Your sacred signature begins to birth a completion energy within you as it begins to transmit out into the Universe. Your signature also flows out and across the earth plane, assisting to anchor a light energy with other human beings on planet earth.

There is a collective energy formed by all of you who have activated your "light signatures." Together, you create a revolutionary unit of love, which creates an expanded dimensional setting within the planet. This pioneering aspect of love is what will make the difference in launching the energy of this New Dawning era. Your collective "light signatures" effectively create a huge awakening light on the earth, supporting many other humans to find their energetic path. This collective energy acts as a magnet to draw those who are ready to join in this energetic emergence. Understand that for many of you this meeting is a pre-agreement.

There is a common element that exists within your sacred signature, which gives you the ability to telepathically align to each other through a communion. When your sacred signature is anchored within your energetic field, you will find that you can transmit an intention through your telepathic center, connecting to all those who have this common element of love. You send out a signal that is felt and recognized by each sacred signature, and you are then drawn to each other through a magnetic light force.

Your essence joins a collective energy that is required to support the anchoring and stabilization within the planet. This collective light assists other human beings to move and align to their awakening process. Remember: As a human being, your awakened energy has the most impact on the transformation of the planet. Other energies within the Universe are supporting, of course, but your transformation contributes the most. As human beings you create a huge wave of light through your resurrection process, which transfers directly to the awakening energy of the planet.

Now is the time for you to create your own sacred light signature through creating your own energetic alignments. This is a simple and natural process done through your Command Energy. As you create three energetic alignments you use a sacred sound into the alignments as you hold them in your Conscious Awareness. The three energetic alignments form a sacred union, interacting and coming together in some way. This connection can be formed either physically or energetically, and this births your sacred signature.

~~~

Beloved Ones,

You stand on the threshold of another turning point as you take this step today and activate these energetic portals. You will find a new depth of you. With just a moment in time, a breath taken, you move your Self into another state of being.

You actually connect to aspects of your Self that have been lying dormant. Now you step forward, with hands outstretched, and you reach for your Self. You receiving you, like a small child taking its first step.

Breathe and move toward the brilliance of your light. Breathe and receive your Self through the portals of light within you. We hold you with love and a great appreciation for all the moments that bring you to now.

Blessings,
The Pleiadians

~~~

Birthing Your New Blueprint Energy

Audio file: Chapter 11
Audio file #1
Sacred sound: ASHA TAE

Now that you have activated your Command Energy you have natural access to your Destiny line. Your bridge is open to access your blueprint for the necessary energetic changes to be made. The Pleiadians have created an energetic container that will birth and then activate your new blueprint energy.

1. Activate your core. This is a very important first step because your core will energetically reflect the changed energy of your blueprint. Bring the palms of your hands together at the center of your heart line (at the sternum). Bring your Conscious Awareness to where the palms meet and take a Conscious Breath. Let go and move into the alignment within your core, the opening. Feel the opening of your core and allow yourself to anchor, like roots of a tree into the earth.

2. You are going to build your core's energy by opening up your Command Energy within the core. Use the sacred sound ASHA TAE. Your Command Energy will expand your core energy. Integrate this expansion of your core.

3. You will be given access to your Destiny line through your portal connection. You will move through the portal to your Destiny line through your Command Energy.

   Begin an alignment to your Command Energy. Do this by aligning to your core. As you open into your expanded core, activate your Command Energy ASHA TAE. Feel or sense your essence build as you expand through your core.

4. Now you are going to access your portal within your heart center. Bring your hands and place your palms on your heart center. Bring your Command Energy into your heart center. Use your Life Force Breath into your heart center. Allow the expansion in your heart center.

5. You are going to bring your Command Energy into your portal. Use ASHA TAE as you do this. Your Destiny line will open within your portal. Bring your full Life Force Breath into your Destiny line and let go. You will be moved. Feel or sense your Self enter an energetic space that holds your current blueprint. Open up to the energy of your blueprint through your Command energy.

Use ASHA TAE if you need to, or you may already be fully aligned to your Command Energy. Open your full consciousness into the essence of your Command Energy and feel the full energy held within your current blueprint. Just let go. As you bring your full Command energy within your blueprint an energetic container forms around your blueprint energy.

6.   Feel the building of your essence within your Command energy. Breathe your Life Force Energy into the opening of the energetic container that has formed to birth your new blueprint energy.

7.   Build your Command Energy into this energetic container. Use ASHA TAE to bring the full force of your Command Energy within the space, filling the space with your conscious energy. Then bring your Life Force Breath into the container. Feel or sense the energy beginning to birth. Keep using your Life Force Breath, working with this creating energy that is forming.

Open up into your full Command Energy essence and witness the full forming of this new blueprint energy. Keep letting go and Being. Allow all that is here for you in this moment. Allow your full experience.

8.   When you feel complete, return to your core position. Your core will be reflecting your new blueprint energy. Integrate through your core and let go. Note: It is important to utilize the earth's energy for a full integration. Lie on the earth and let go.

Opening Into Your Sacred Trust

Audio file: Chapter 11
Audio file #2
Sacred sound: ASHA TAE

1.   Bring both hands to connect to your heart center. Use your conscious Life Force Breath to expand your connection to your heart. Anchor your Command Energy through your heart space. Use the sacred sound ASHA TAE.

2.   Now you are going to access your portal within your heart center. Bring your Command Energy into the opening of your portal. Use your Life Force Breath into your portal. Feel or sense the activation within your portal.

3. You are going to bring your Command Energy deeper into the portal. Use ASHA TAE; as you do this your Destiny line will open within your portal. Bring your full Life Force Breath into your Destiny line, and let go. You will moved onto the bridge.

4. Open into your telepathic center by bringing your right hand upward to open into your telepathic center. Bring your Conscious Awareness into the energy of your hand position and then follow the line of energy into the opening of your telepathic center. Take your time opening into the energy of your center. Breathe and let go.

5. Bring your consciousness into the Code Form and wait for your telepathic center to absorb the Code Form. You are going to work with the Code Form for sacred trust (see Diagram N).

6. Now place the Code Form from your telepathic center on to the bridge. You do this by bringing your telepathic connection to the bridge and waiting for the bridge to absorb the Code Form. Your bridge on your Destiny line will recognize the Code Form, which acts like a key to a door. The doorway opens into your sacred trust.

Diagram N

7. Your doorway to your sacred trust is open, but you need to enter with your Command Energy. Take time to activate your Command Energy and align fully to your essence. Use ASHA TAE.

8. You enter the doorway with your Command Essence and bring your full consciousness to the doorway. Then use your Life Force Breath, breathing into the doorway. This moves you into the energy of your sacred trust.

9. Align to your Command Energy and use ASHA TAE. Then stretch your right arm forward with the palm of your hand and fingers spread wide open, almost as though you are reaching inside a bag to receive something. As you enter your sacred trust to receive, align more fully into your Command Energy and use ASHA TAE.

    Then bring your Conscious Awareness to your hand and open up to receive what is here for you. Just let go and allow. Remember: Breathe into what is given to you. Unwrap the gift by touching it with your Conscious Awareness and using your Life Force Breath.

10. When you are complete bring your hand straight back toward you. Link your hand into your solar plexus; the heel of your hand connects into your solar plexus. The energy from your sacred trust will integrate through your solar plexus and then into your energetic field.

11. Come back into your heart center with both hands connecting. Bring all aspects of your Conscious Awareness into your heart. Integrate. Take all the time you need to allow a full integration.

Working With the Natural Forces

Audio file: Chapter 11
Audio file #3
Sacred sound: ASHA TAE
Sacred sound: EE

Remember: First choose with what you are going connect to in nature, then begin your process.

1. Activate your core. This is a very important first step whenever you work with the natural forces. A strong anchoring of the core will support you in moving deeply into all the multi-dimensional energies with the world of the natural forces and remaining stable. It will help you anchor as you are working within the levels of your Command Energy within your telepathic center. Take the time you need to allow a full birthing and anchoring through your core before you go to the next step.

   Bring the palms of your hands together at the center of your heart line (at the sternum). Bring your Conscious Awareness to where the palms meet and take a Conscious Breath. Let go and move into the alignment within your core, the opening. Feel the opening of your core and allow yourself to anchor, like roots of a tree into the earth.

2. Move your hands and place them on your heart center. Feel your connection to your heart center and bring your Conscious Awareness into your heart. Use your life force to connect into your heart cells. Then bring your consciousness into the portal within your heart. Use your sound EE to open into your portal. This aligns you to your natural connection to your Command Energy.

3. Bring your right hand upward to open into your telepathic center. Bring your Conscious Awareness into the energy of your hand

position and then follow the line of energy into the opening of your telepathic center. Take your time opening into the energy of your telepathic center. Breathe and let go.

4. Begin to build your Command Energy. Use your sacred sound ASHA TAE. Feel or sense your energy build. Feel or sense your connection within your telepathic center expand in some way.

5. Bring the palm of your right hand forward to connect to the nature form you have chosen. Remember: All connection to nature is through your telepathic communion center. Bring your Command Energy toward the nature form, and allow the connection.

6. Just let go into your experience. Allow your full opening within all aspects of yourself and at the same time, you begin to open into all aspects of the nature form.

   Use your Life Force Breath and breathe into this re-union taking place. This will expand the communion energy. Keep letting go. It is through letting go that you can align even more into your experience. Note: If it feels right you can build another level of your Command Energy. Use ASHA TAE during this connection with the nature form.

7. When you are ready, gently disengage from the communion with the nature form by bringing your Command Energy and Conscious Awareness back to your hand. Then disconnect the telepathic center by bringing your right hand down.

8. Bring your hands on to your heart center and bring all of your Conscious Awareness into your heart. Use your Life Force Breath to integrate the energy from the interaction to the natural forces.

9. Come back to your core position and allow a full integration of these multi-dimensional expansions. Take all the time you need to allow a full integration.

Creating Your Energetic Alignments

Audio file: Chapter 11
Audio file #4
Sacred sound: ASHA TAE
Sacred sound: EE SHAH

You will create your energetic alignment with your Command Energy. You will be utilizing your Command Energy to birth these sacred alignments and these alignments will generate automatic adjustments throughout your system. Note: As you birth three energetic alignments they will form a sacred signature within them that will anchor within your energetic field.

1. Activate your core. This is a very important first step whenever you work within creating energetic alignments. A strong anchoring of the core will support you in being able to move deeply into all the energies within your energetic field and create these alignments.

   Bring the palms of your hands together at the center of your heart line (at the sternum). Bring your Conscious Awareness to where the palms meet and take a Conscious Breath. Let go and move into the alignment within your core, the opening. Feel the opening of your core and allow yourself to anchor, like roots of a tree into the earth.

2. You are going to create an infinity movement within your heart space. The palms of your hands are together and you begin to move your hands from your central position of the sternum. Create the infinity movement out sideways from the central position, and then cross back through the central sternum position to the other side to complete your infinity movement. Complete it back at your core position. This movement will birth an expanded dimensional space through your core. Look at the design of the infinity movement shown in Diagram O. Note: You can start on either side, left or right. It does not matter.

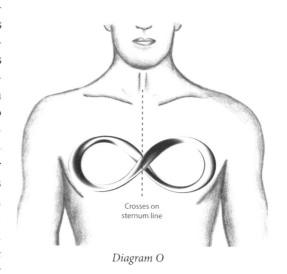

Crosses on sternum line

Diagram O

3. Back at your core position, integrate the dimensional energy within your core. Bring your Conscious Awareness into your core, breathe, and let go.

4. Bring your Conscious Awareness out into your energetic field. You are going to build your Command Energy through your energetic field. You will do this until you feel or sense you have enough Command Energy to build your first energetic alignment. Use your sacred sound ASHA TAE.

5. Bring the palms of your hands out into your energetic field facing

upward, and bring your consciousness into your palms. As you do this, your Command Energy will begin to flow toward you and into your hands. You will feel, sense, or see the energy that has been formed moving into your hands.

6.   Work with your Command Energy to create the energetic alignment. Use your Life Force Breath, your hands, and your Conscious Awareness to work with the energy that you have created through your Command Energy sound. You may see, sense, or feel this energetic alignment as it is created.

7.   When this alignment feels complete you are going to anchor the alignment. Use the sacred sound EE SHAH. Place the sound into your energetic alignment, and this will anchor your alignment in your energetic field. Witness your energetic alignment shift its energetic form as it anchors.

8.   Now come back to your heart center, both hands connecting through the palms on to your heart. Feel the energy expand into the heart. Bring your Command Energy into building this heart connection. Use ASHA TAE.

9.   Move your Command Energy essence back to the energetic alignment within your energetic field. Bring your Life Force Breath into the alignment; feel or sense the transformation of the alignment.

10. Bring your Command Energy back to your heart center. This creates a pathway between the energetic alignment and your heart. Integrate through your heart. Take all the time you need to allow a full integration.

To Birth Your Sacred Signature

1.   You first need to create three energetic alignments as described previously.

2.   Bring your Conscious Awareness to all three energetic alignments within your energetic field and use the sound ANAE SHEAN until all three alignments have formed a united flow among them or possibly birthed into one form.

3.   Anchor your sacred signature with the sound EE SHAH. Your sacred signature is now activated through your energetic field. Know that as you birth your sacred signature you activate a wave of light through the Universe and throughout the earth plane. Your unique light pattern impacts all life force within the Universe, including all human beings and planet Earth.

12

Aligning to Your Sacred Flow, Re-United to Your Place

As I sit down to write this final chapter I am deeply moved by the Pleiadians sharing with me what they need to relate to you at this time. It brought me to a place of questioning myself: *Can I do this? Am I capable of imparting this in a way that you will be able to receive it and understand the full importance of this step?* I feared my inability to transfer onto paper what the Pleiadians are giving to me through thought transference. As I let go, my prayer is that I have created the weaving with words that enable you to fully comprehend the message.

This is a grand adventure that you have taken on in this lifetime, a story that within our dimensional realms takes but a moment to complete. When you created your design—your story that you were going to live out here on the earth plane—you set it in motion from the dimensional realms reality, not the reality of the third-dimensional plane.

You placed within your story everything you wanted to experience and everything you needed to experience for your next step, so you could gain understanding of this time and take part in this huge awakening on your earth plane. You chose the individuals to have experiences with and they chose you. You made pre-agreements between each other to learn through the interactions that you would bring to each other. You celebrated these pre-agreements before you came here.

You also made other pre-agreements for this time. These pre-agreements held different energies for a different purpose. They involved a mutual connection and commitment for the completion of a specific mission on this earth plane, at this time of the New Dawning. They involved the pre-agreements of other human beings, yes. More important was the one pre-agreement you made with a certain "life force energy" or a collective group of life force energies from the Collective Universe. Examples of some of the possible pre-agreement energies are the Spiritual energies, Angels, Light Beings, and Masters. Others include pre-agreements with the alien forces—for example, the Pleiadians, the Serians, and the Star energies. For some of you it included the Lemurians and Atlantians.

With the assistance from this pre-agreement energy you were going to move into a "completion cycle" and then return to your place within the Universal Grid. You would stay on the earth plane to have your human experience, and at the same time be consciously aligned to your divine spiritual aspect within your place on the Universal Grid. This is your pre-agreement mission to accomplish in this lifetime!

Why is this particular pre-agreement so necessary? Part of your mission here is to reach a point where you will need to work alongside an energetic alliance in order to support your human self's evolution to a "completion energy." This was the design so you could ultimately learn the lessons of communion with your human aspect. As your human aspect transformed within this communion experience with your energetic alliance, there would simultaneously be a communion forged between your divine aspect and your human self, ending the separation within your human aspect.

I am not talking about a "perfect" communion relationship; this is not necessary. Just the experience of a communion moment with your human aspect and Self is enough. In that moment, the separation between the human aspect and Self comes to an end. Within that moment, which is really timeless, there is a sacred anchoring that births into the cells of your body. You claim and anchor your place back home on the Universal Grid. You help to complete the picture for your Self and the Universe.

This was your design for this pre-agreement, to assist your human aspect to transform into some of the fourth/fifth-dimensional aspects of experience.

Remember the completion energy? This included your human aspect changing the relationship with the Self. Moving from a third-dimensional relationship of self-condemnation of the ego mind, into a fourth/fifth-dimensional relationship through the heart, created this transformed alignment within your Self. You are moving to a place of self-love, compassion, patience, and awakening into living consciously as the sacred divine aspect of the Self. At the same time you can continue to have your human experience, making mistakes, and being vulnerable, all of this while being awakened.

Your enlightenment process depends on the end of separation between your human aspect and your awakened divine aspect of Self. There must be an experience of Oneness between these aspects so that you have this direct experience within the cells of your body. This creates a completion energy on a certain level.

Now you have nearly come back home to a place of remembering. You have done your work to bring your Self to a place of self-resurrection. The time is close when there will be a completion for many of you. However, there are still some important steps for you to take, and they hold subtle realizations that you need to be willing to receive. To hear them and then to actually Be with them. To understand a concept is not enough. You must be open to the concept and make it alive through a direct experience. Only then is it reawakened through you, within your cells.

You are now consciously working with your Command Energy. You need the support of your Command Energy to connect to the energetic alliance with which you have made a pre-agreement. This is your next step, moving toward experiencing a moment of Oneness with your human aspect.

As this experience of Oneness with Self awakens in you, you can hold the platform for the rest of the planet, because you carry the direct experience within your cells and energetic field. Just one moment of this experience of Oneness anchors it through your cells and in your energetic field. Each moment of experience is cumulative, so each successive moment of experiencing Oneness becomes easier. Your experience also helps those who follow you to transform this aspect of their humanness. Then as each human transforms in this way the platform can grow.

You see, no one can help you with this piece. Your energetic alliances cannot hold the platform because they are not human. Only you, who holds the human aspect within you, those who have made a pre-agreement to hold this platform for the rest of the human race, can do so by opening into this direct experience of Oneness.

Many of you are ready for this step in your transformation. Up to this point in time, your main focus has been on your spiritual awakening. Now is the time to bring the focus on your human aspect in order for you to experience a moment of sacred communion. This experience of communion creates an energetic setting to enable your human part to have an experience of a sacred union. Each communion experience anchors the essence of Oneness within the cells of your body. This anchoring of Oneness in the cells allows the human aspect of you and the sacred Self to meet beyond the third-dimensional illusion.

I would like to share my story with you, a moment of Oneness with my human aspect: Mother Mary was my pre-agreement alliance. I was visiting one of her sacred sites where she had appeared many times. This is one of my most favorite places to be on the planet. I was sitting in a tiny chapel where she had appeared many years ago. On the wall was a painted picture of Mary transmitting energy through her eyes into aliens; to me they had the energy of the Pleiadians. Then I could feel her transmitting into me. She spoke directly to my human aspect and said, "You still have your Self on the cross!"

I was surprised because I thought I had let go of my self-condemnation. A part of me knew she was right—I was still holding aspects from my past. All of a sudden everything began to fall away from me. I could see my cross burning and there was no going back. In that moment I experienced the whole of my life playing out, all the parts that I had played and all the players, including myself. In that moment I moved into a place of self-love, joy, and gratitude for all that I had been through, and for everyone who played their role. I moved into a state of Oneness with Mary, reuniting with her.

That full experience is anchored in my cells. I can move into that experience at any time, and as I share this with you now I can feel the joy and freedom bubbling up inside of me. That's what Spirit means by each moment being timeless. I am free, and I have fully experienced and anchored my moment of Oneness. Does it mean I am in that state all of the time? No. However, I have not been the same since then, and this is because in that moment my human aspect and divine aspect forged a union that never breaks.

Through my human interaction with Mother Mary I was able to anchor that moment of sacred union in the cells of my body. This led me to re-join with my sacred aspect of Self because my human aspect moved out of the third-dimensional experience with Mother Mary. This allowed me the possibility of meeting my sacred Self on the fourth/fifth-dimensional level, ending an element of separation between my humanness and aspect of Self.

This allowed me to begin a new journey within my human experience. I was able to let go of many old hurts, old concepts, and was able to appreciate a deeper level of love for myself. In turn, this allowed me to expand compassion toward myself and also to extend that compassion and love to others. I gained a greater understanding of the journey, and through that clarity I was able to engage with my divine Self, deepening that connection. Each time we had moments of connection my transformation led me to a greater self-love.

So it is with great love and a deep gratitude that I move forward with each one of you here on your journey. Know that I hold the platform of this completion journey for each one of you, and it is my deep wish for you to join me in holding this essential platform for the others who will follow you.

Let's begin to look at the processes the Pleiadians have developed in order for you to connect back to the energy of the pre-agreement that you made to take this next step. This is important for you to experience. It allows you to fully let go and just move forward with your plan. The Pleiadians tell me that they have designed an energetic setting within a Chamber to take you back to the moment you anchored this specific energetic pre-agreement. It is time for you to activate this pre-agreement with this energetic alliance and then move into the next step of your design.

Are you ready to work with this first process? Know that you can call on my support with each step if it feels supportive. You will be working with your Command Energy initially to enter the energetic space within the Chamber. You will be working through your telepathic communion center to communicate with your pre-agreement alliance energy. You will have another level of support in this special mission journey with your pre-agreement energetic alliance; they are committed to you through each step of this process. Your portal will be expanding to a new dimensional setting to allow you to open into this pre-agreement connection.

You will be calling on your human aspect to witness and then participate in this communion connection to the pre-agreement alliance energy.

Aligning to the Energetic Chamber

Audio file: Chapter 12
Audio file #1
Sacred sound: ASHA TAE
Sacred sound: EE

1. Bring both hands to connect to your heart center. Use your conscious Life Force Breath to expand your connection to your heart. Anchor your Command Energy through your heart space using the sound ASHA TAE. Allow the expansion and receive your heart consciously. So right now begin an alignment to your Command Energy as you claim your heart.

2. Now you are going to access your portal within your heart center. Bring your Command Energy into the opening of your portal. Use your Life Force Breath into your portal. Feel the activation within your portal. Then use the sound EE into your portal. Feel or sense another opening here. Let go as the energy within your portal opens. Use your Life Force Breath and place it fully into the portal. This expansion of your portal is designed to support you in the Chamber.

3. You are going to activate your Command Energy through the portal, using ASHA TAE. As you do this, your Destiny line will open within your portal. Bring your full Life Force Breath into your Destiny line, and let go. You will be moved, feel, or sense your Self within the Chamber. This Chamber holds the energy of the Light Council. You find yourself within the circle of the Light Council.

4. Open into your telepathic center by bringing your right hand upward to open into your telepathic center. Bring your Conscious Awareness into the energy of your hand position. Then follow the line of energy into the opening of your telepathic center. Take your time opening into the energy of your center. Breathe and let go.

5. Open up into your Command Energy and use your sound ASHA TAE. Then bring your right hand upward to connect within a telepathic communion toward the Light Council. Feel them transmit to you the energies of your pre-agreement with this energetic alliance before you came to the earth plane. Use your Life Force Breath to open into this pre-agreement energy. Let go. Take your time to feel, see, or sense this energy. It's important to allow your full experience and to take in all the energies that are being presented to you.

6. You are being asked to activate that pre-agreement now. You do this by using your Command Energy and anchoring it into this circle. You will be witnessed as you activate this pre-agreement. Use ASHA TAE until the pre-agreement feels completed in the activation.

    You may or not be aware of the identity of this energetic alliance. If you do know it, then do not question the identity. In this setting you are not able to imagine someone, so it is the correct identity. Note: If you are not ready to activate this pre-agreement that is okay. This is your journey and in saying no you will be honored and respected.

7. When you feel fully integrated by the activation of your pre-agreement you will place your hands on your heart center and bring your awareness into heart. Integrate well, and let go. Allow the full integration of your journey through your heart center.

Aligning to Your Pre-Agreement Alliance Energy

Audio file: Chapter 12
Audio file #2
Sacred sound: ASHA TAE
Sacred sound: EE
Code Form A

You will now align to the energy with which you made the pre-agreement. You will be working with a Code Form that will bring you into a direct connection with your pre-agreement alliance. This is important for you to telepathically connect with your energetic alliance, so that you can take your next step.

1. Bring both hands to connect to your heart center. Use your conscious Life Force Breath to expand your connection to your heart. Anchor your Command Energy through your heart space and use the sound ASHA TAE. Allow the expansion and receive your heart consciously (*this is my heart*). Begin an alignment to your Command Energy as you claim your heart.

2. Now you are going to access your portal within your heart center. Bring your Command Energy into your opening of your portal. Use your Life Force Breath into your portal. Feel the activation within your portal.

    Then use the sound EE into your portal. Feel or sense another opening here. Let go as the energy within your portal opens. Use your Life Force Breath and place it fully into the portal. This expansion of your portal is designed to support you in the Chamber.

3. You are going to activate your Command Energy through the portal, using ASHA TAE. As you do this, your Destiny line will open within your portal. Bring your full Life Force Breath into your Destiny line, and let go. You will be moved, feel, or sense your Self within the Chamber. This chamber holds the energy of the Light Council. You find yourself within the circle of the Light Council.

4. Open into your telepathic center by bringing your right hand upward to open into your telepathic center. Bring your Conscious Awareness into the energy of your hand position and then follow the line of energy into the opening of your telepathic center. Take your time opening into the energy of your center. Breathe and let go.

5. You are going to work with the Code Form A (shown in Diagram P). Bring your consciousness into the Code Form A and wait for your telepathic center to absorb the Code Form.

Diagram P

6. Now place the Code Form A from your telepathic center within the circle of the Light Council. You do this by bringing your telepathic connection into the circle and wait until the Code Form A is absorbed within the circle. This is going to bring to you the energetic essence with which you had a pre-agreement.

7. Open up into your Command Energy. Use your sound ASHA TAE. Then bring your right hand upward to connect within a telepathic communion toward your energetic alliance with whom you made this pre-agreement to help your human aspect have a communion experience. Just let go and allow the re-union. You can use your Life Force Breath to help you integrate the energy of this meeting. Allow a full communion and telepathic communication between you.

8. When you feel fully integrated from this meeting you will place your hands on your heart center and bring your awareness into your heart. Integrate well, and let go. Allow the full integration of your journey through your heart center.

Working With Your Code Forms to Birth Communion With Your Energetic Alliance

Audio file: Chapter 12
Audio file #3
Sacred sound: ASHA TAE
Sacred sound: EE
Code Form A, B, C, D.

You will be working with your Code Forms through your chosen energetic alliance. Note: This energetic alliance is energy with which you had a pre-agreement to help you form communion with your human aspect. You will be working with a series of four Code Forms, each one holding the energies of Oneness/communion. Each one of the Code Forms holds different levels of the initiating frequencies to support the human aspect to experience Oneness.

Your alliance energy will be working closely with you to open this direct experience for your human aspect. You are going to working within the Chamber. It is important for you to just relax and open to the support from your pre-agreed support alliance. Note: You may need many journeys to complete this initiation. Just allow and Be.

1. Bring both hands to connect to your heart center. Use your conscious Life Force Breath to expand your connection to your heart. Anchor your Command Energy through your heart space using the sound ASHA TAE. Allow the expansion and receive your heart consciously (*this is my heart*). Begin an alignment to your Command Energy as you claim your heart.

2. Now you are going to access your portal within your heart center. Bring your Command Energy into your opening of your portal. Use your Life Force Breath into your portal. Feel the activation within your portal.

   Then use the sound EE into your portal, feel, or sense another opening here. Let go as the energy within your portal opens. Use your Life Force Breath and place it fully into the portal. This expansion of your portal is designed to support you in the Chamber.

3. You are going to activate your Command Energy through the portal, using ASHA TAE. As you do this, your Destiny line will open within your portal. Bring your full Life Force Breath into your Destiny line, and let go. You will be moved, feel, or sense your Self within the Chamber. The Chamber holds light energy. This will support you in your initiation. Open fully into the light. Use your Command Energy to assist you in opening fully here. Use ASHA TAE.

4. Open into your telepathic center by bringing your right hand upward to open into your telepathic center. Bring your Conscious Awareness into the energy of your hand position and then follow the line of energy into the opening of your telepathic center. Take your time opening into the energy of your center. Breathe and let go. As you move into your telepathic center open into the light of the Chamber, allow the communion with the light.

5. You are going to work with the Code Form A shown in Diagram P. Bring your consciousness into the Code Form A and wait for your telepathic center to absorb the Code Form.

6. Now place the Code Form from your telepathic center within the Chamber. This will call forth your energetic alliance. You do this

by bringing your telepathic connection into the Chamber and wait until the Code Form A is absorbed, received by your alliance energy. Open up your telepathic communion toward your alliance energy when you begin to perceive their presence. Allow the connection.

7. Open up into your Command Energy and use your sound ASHA TAE. Then bring your right hand upward to connect within a telepathic communion toward your energetic alliance, with whom you made this pre-agreement to assist your human aspect to have a communion experience. Just let go and allow the reunion. You can use your Life Force Breath to help you integrate the energy of this meeting. Allow a full communion and telepathic communication between you.

8. You are now going to start working with Code Forms B, C, and D (see Diagram Q on page 155). Each of these code forms holds different elements of initiation that will help you form a sacred communion with your energetic alliance. Let's look at the steps for activation and working with these three initiating Code Forms. You always start with the Code Form B and then C and then D.

   Step 1: First, you are going to work with the Code Form B (Diagram Q on page 155). Bring your consciousness into the Code Form B, and wait for your telepathic center to absorb the Code Form.

   Step 2: Bring your full consciousness into your telepathic center. Feel or sense the Code Form begin to expand within your telepathic communion center. Use your Life Force Breath to expand into the initiation.

   Step 3: Open up into your Command Energy and use your sound ASHA TAE. Then bring your right hand upward to connect within a telepathic communion toward your energetic alliance. Let go into the connection. Integrate this communion connection through your cells. Let go. You will do steps 1, 2, and 3 with each of the three Code Forms, B, C, and D. It is important to work with all three Code Forms in one process.

9. When you feel fully integrated from these Code Form initiations you will place your hands on your heart center and bring your Conscious Awareness into your heart. Integrate well, and let go. Allow the full integration of your journey through your heart center.

Remember: Do not try to assess these initiations. Simply keep letting go and allowing moments within the initiations for your human aspect to be present.

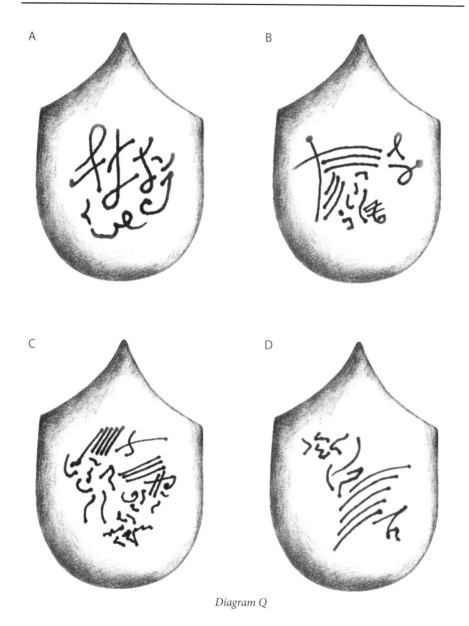

Diagram Q

No perfection here. It is simply a moment in time of sacred communion/One-ness. Just focus on letting go and allowing the energy of each Code Form to simply move you to another place within the communion to your energetic alliance.

~~~

Beloved Ones,

We greet you. In this moment of time we ask you to open up to the energies that are being held for you now. Now is the time to step forward to receive many gifts. These gifts are yours by divine birthright. They are being made available to you now because you need them. You have said yes to being here at this time. You have said yes to a journey of divine proportions so that you take your place within the Collective Consciousness/the Oneness.

You have a place within the Oneness. To claim this place consciously is so essential at this time. As you claim your place on a conscious level a door can open and you can walk through this doorway. We hold this doorway open with tremendous love and respect for all that you are in this moment.

Know that you are "perfectly imperfect" in your humanness in this moment. There is nothing that you need to change about yourself in order to be received within this light wheel on the Universal Grid. Take a breath and claim yourself within your humanness. Hold your Self with love and deep appreciation for your journey and all that you have lived up to this point of time.

Our role is to bring the fifth-dimensional energy of unconditional love to each one of you as you fulfill your destiny. We are here to assist, simply to hold the love. Be still and know the truth of this within your heart. Walk through the doorway and take your place.

Blessings,
The Pleiadians

~~~

Appendix A:

Questions and Answers

Chapter 1

Q: Why do you think that "the fall" and the separation happened in the first place?

C: Well, we came here and we entered the earth plane in separation; we came here because we weren't complete, and we were going to have to move through this whole new process of being human, of consciously being human and birthing our spiritual natures at the same time. So we all set a plan in place of how we would come into this earth plane, the experiences we would have as children, the experiences we would have in our lives, and those experiences in third dimension, in that illusion, slowly shut us down from remembering who we were. Then we had to make the journey back. That was part of the plan.

At the same time we had that plan, there was the New Dawning age, and we all agreed to be here at this time to go through this process and go through this revolution. It's really a revolutionary time for the whole Universe.

Q: What do you think is revolutionary about it?

C: It's revolutionary because it's the very first time in the Universe that there has been an active awakening of the transformation of a planet and a third-dimensional illusion being broken away and a fourth/fifth-dimensional coming into place while we're still human and having a human experience—with those vulnerabilities—but birthing consciously and waking up while still being in our human aspect. That's why it's revolutionary.

Q: And will we have any memory of the old?

C: You'll have a memory, but you won't be able to hang on to it because you'll be out of the drama of the third dimension. You're into drama in the third dimension, big time. You'll just remember. There won't be emotional attachments or triggers connected to your past, and you won't be holding on to anything.

You'll be seeing it is a play on a stage, a play you took part in with all the other players, and you were one of the players to have your experience, and that is just simply the truth. And when that occurs, when you get to that place, you'll say, "Oh, I played my part, and so did everybody else." You all pre-agreed to play your part together. It's that simple.

I had the direct experience of this, and nothing was ever the same again because everything let go, and that's when I went into another state of being. The moment I became and had the full experience of being just a player on the stage and everybody else played their part, everything let go. That's when my cross burned, because I was no longer emotionally connected to it.

So that's just part of the process you move through when you're ready. Once you start the self-loving process, it all leaves and you're just a player on the stage, and there's nothing left except love for yourself and everybody else.

This is really what you need to start working with. You have been doing the best you could in the moment and having your experience. And when you get down to that, there's really nothing left. You can allow yourself to hold yourself to that love, and it becomes a natural state. You don't even have to think about it anymore. It simply is. And so is everybody else. And that's where you're moving. To me, it is really beautiful. You can get a head start on this. Every one of you has quite a bit of work to do. You have a mission to hold a space, a platform, for the rest of the world so they can come into this the way they need to, and you have said yes to doing it this way.

It took a lot of courage to say yes to your journey, because it's not an easy transition the way you're doing it. But it's glorious once you leave all the stuff behind, and we're all here together. We're not separated. And that's what you get when the love starts to come through. It's so important that you start letting yourself consider the idea of moving back to this new relationship with your human Self.

Q: I feel a huge difficulty dealing with my pride, arrogance. What can I do?

C: Honor this and know this about yourself. You know that you have this arrogance, right? So you honor it and smile and say, "Okay, here I go again" and you breathe. You can say, "All right, I am changing this in this moment. I feel the arrogance. I hold myself with love." You are so afraid you need to be arrogant. Arrogance usually comes from a fear that you are not okay, but it is really okay. I'm going to love you. I know you are afraid and I love you.

And love will start shifting the part that is arrogant to feel loved and okay. The next time you feel the arrogance coming, you look at the situation and ask yourself what you are afraid of. Hold yourself with love and say, "It's okay; it's really okay and I love you."

Gradually there is transformation, but in the meantime you accept your arrogance. Know it is part of your vulnerability; know it is connected to something about fear. Don't make a big deal about it. It is human. It is imperfect.

Q: Is this what we are doing here?

C: When you are willing just to love who you are, the evolution accelerates. The divine aspect of yourself is all loving; it loves you completely. Every time you choose to love yourself, your humanness, the divine aspect can enter more of you.

Q: And on another plane, do we have more awareness of this?

C: Yes, out of the third dimension. What happens when you start loving this aspect is you start living more in the other planes because with love; you are not separating anymore. You are accepting and it's not about perfection; it's accepting your humanness, so the separation ends inside of you. When you end the separation through acceptance, not perfection, you move into the fourth/fifth dimension. In the past you've been told that you have to be perfect in order to become enlightened. This is not true. This has been a lie to keep you locked into separation here. This truth is absolutely glorious; it's liberating, and you liberate yourselves. No one can do it for anyone else. It's simple and it's glorious.

Chapter 2

Q: How do you start this Conscious Choice with pre-agreements?

C: Start with what you need in your life or what is in front of you right now. You can ask for clarity on the pre-agreement and you can allow it to unfold. It's a relationship; all you are doing is allowing a relationship to unfold with the spiritual realms and you are moving into that now as they are naturally aligned to you. We are all part of the God essence, so part of the New Dawning energy is that, in your daily lives, you have a natural connection with Spirit, the Angels, and the Aliens. You all live in a certain harmony and unity of Oneness.

Q: What do you do with your pre-agreements?

C: You develop a relationship with the team and, as you need their support, it is there. You speak to them and tell them what it is you need, what's going on right now, and it unfolds. You don't have to be specific to start, but you do need to start building and connecting to these relationships.

The idea of the pre-agreements is that you are going to have a relationship with the spiritual realms or the energetic alliances that you have called forth. This develops your telepathic ability, and every time you use your telepathic communication you birth another level of light frequency through the cells of your body. When you utilize the gifts that you have been given your enlightenment process accelerates. That's why this is a very important piece.

Q: If one person in the "partnership" is doing this work and not the other, is it enough for one person to call this pre-agreement into being?

C: If the other person isn't really honoring the pre-agreements to do the work on him- or herself then he or she can't carry the essence of the project and you had a pre-agreement for the two of you to hold the energetic platform together. It's an energy that you carry when you have a project or a mission. Sometimes that person drops out and a new person comes in because it requires more than one. My feeling is that you are going to have to move away from this person and have a new one come if the other person has made a decision not to fulfill the contract.

Q: Is it possible to get more specific about what is coming?

C: Well, there is just a lot of upheaval. We know that there is this energy, this third-dimensional energy shifting and a fourth/fifth-dimensional energy of light coming onto the planet, so there is a lot of energetic friction. But there are some intense earth changes coming that are going to create physical upheaval in the earth. It's going to also create some hardship for human beings to live as you used to live or in the way you are living now.

So you need to align to your divine natures and work from that space. There may be chaos around, but the drama and chaos don't have to be within you. You can stay stable within yourself and anchor energy with your pre-agreed team. This can help anchor and stabilize energy on the earth plane and help you work with what is taking place on the earth.

Q: How do we help our loved ones?

C: By being stable within yourself. By being a light that holds an element of peace and stability. And everyone will have their own experience. You cannot save them from their drama. They need the drama. If they are in the drama, they need the drama. You can share, you can bring forth information, but you cannot save your children from their experiences, nor should you, because they have come here to have their experience. They too have said yes to being on the earth plane, just like you have. Children are coming in with a very strong awareness right now.

Allow the divine aspects to guide you and take you through, even though you don't know where you are going to end up. You know it's right, and the rightness in the moment is everything. There is nothing more you need to know other than being in the moment. Even if you think you know, you don't, so rest in that.

Chapter 3

Q: Can you talk more about the crystalline structure?

C: The crystalline structure is electrical in nature and it rewires all of your systems to carry a higher voltage of light in the cells. The cells actually get rewired and the electrical form births through you so you can carry a high voltage of your own light in this body now. That's the idea of the crystalline structure coming in at this time.

How else are you going to align to the new dimensional energy that is birthing on the planet? Eventually, fourth/fifth/sixth-dimensional energy will be fully aligned on this planet.

Q: If someone doesn't consciously choose to activate the crystalline structure, can it or will it still become activated?

C: When this earth plane moves completely into fourth/fifth dimension it will be in instant activation for those human beings who already have it there and have not had it activated. That is the only way they will be able to stay on the earth plane.

Q: Is the crystalline structure physical within our bodies?

C: You are actually going through a crystalline re-structuring. The crystalline structure is in the space between the cells of the body. Science is even finding a change in the crystalline structure within our bodies. It means our organs will transform eventually and this is just the first level of crystalline structure that has been anchored in us. There are many levels that will anchor.

Q: A lot of people are having physical symptoms. I've had this vibrating at the top of my head. Would that be part of the physical changes?

C: Yes, that's part of it. Your brain is going through a transformation. You are actually beginning to open up a new level of your brain, and you're going to start working from that. That is the awakening. Part of evolving and awakening to yourselves, is this aspect of your brain opening up.

Some of the remembrance will come from this area of the brain, remembering who you are and your connections.

Q: Can you speak about where we're going as a fifth-dimension or fourth-dimension being, say, evolving out of the carbon-based bodies into silicon-based bodies? What sort of body do you think we will have?

C: They will be crystalline structures.

Q: Will we be light bodies?

C: No. You are still going to remain in your human form, but your cells will transform. Understand: There's a transmitter within each cell that has been lying dormant for lifetimes. You were birthed with it inside, but it has never been activated, and that transmitter is being activated now by this new birthing frequency that's coming onto the earth.

As you transform dimensionally to the fourth/fifth dimension, the transmitter activates a signal of your divine frequency, but it's not just transmitting it out into the Universe. It's transmitting it through the organs and the cells of your body, transforming the structures. That's why you're going to start living longer. You're going through a transformation of your cells right now. They've already begun to change.

Everybody who is on this earth plane is going to go through this transformation. Those who are consciously awake right now will go through it first, and then hold an energetic space for the others to transform. These are the "way-showers."

You are receiving these downloaded energies right now. Every time there's an earthquake and there's a fourth/fifth-dimensional shift on the planet, your Self is going through this transformation. Every time.

It has to be slow because you need to adjust to the energies that are taking place, but that's why you're able to align with the earth plane and with the natural forces, because the actual cellular structure is transmuting, and that allows us to communicate very differently on a very different level than ever before.

You're all going through it. That's why people are having a tremendous amount of illnesses. Strange things are happening to people's thyroids, for example, because of the changes that are taking place in the physical body.

The earth is going to go through a complete regeneration, too. It's going to be totally transformed and hold a whole new frequency that it hasn't had in lifetimes. It's actually going to be re-established back into a whole new level of consciousness and light, and it's going to just be in a new state when this is complete. And you are going to be in a new state also.

Q: Like we think of miracles happening?

C: Well, miracles you think of are third-dimensional miracles, but fourth/fifth-dimension, miracles—they're not miracles. They're just the state of those dimensional spaces. It's natural. A natural realignment is going to occur, and is occurring.

Q: You said the crystalline structure anchored into every human being on this planet on 11/11/11. Are there those who would have not have chosen that?

C: You have all pre-agreed to be on this earth plane to receive this crystalline structure. At that time every human being wherever they are on the planet now (whether they remember or not) made a pre-agreement to be here at this time for this change.

The crystalline structure anchored, but it did not get activated and it hasn't been activated yet on many, many levels. You have to activate the crystalline structure through conscious choice.

Q: So that is the choice?

C: Yes, that is a choice. There is going to come a time on the planet when it will go purely to a fourth/fifth-dimensional structure and the third-dimensional illusion will drop away. The crystalline structure in everybody will activate at that time and support every human being that is here, even those who are not spiritually awake.

There will be people on this earth plane who are into violence, control, killing; those people will not be staying on this earth plane at a certain point. Everyone here on this earth plane, regardless of who they are, will be taking their next steps; some will stay on the planet taking their next steps, and some will not align to the fourth/fifth-dimensional energies. These people are not ready for that awakening, and they will step off the planet to their next step. There is always a next step.

There is no such thing as death. The Pleiadians say we are all just taking a next step here or a step there. They are very matter-of-fact about it.

There are a lot people who are not spiritually awake who are meant to be on the planet and are staying here through the changes. You don't have to be spiritual to be here on the planet. There is not going to be this huge mass exodus of people who are non-spiritual. The people who are ready to take that step and who are not into control or power or violence will stay and they will move.

People like you end up being the "way-showers." You have made pre-agreements to wake up before a lot of others and you will hold energetic spaces for the other people who will be coming behind you. You will have forged a pathway, and they will come into their awakening and you will be the support for them.

Q: What if I don't have a thyroid?

C: You still have the energetic blueprint of your thyroid and the crystalline structure is not third dimensional. It is fourth/fifth dimensional, so it is perfectly there.

Q: With missing parts of the body, is the "blueprint" missing, too?

C: It's always in the body. Part of the regeneration that's going to be taking place in the body is the organs re-growing themselves from that blueprint.

Q: They are going to re-grow themselves?

C: Yes, they will. And they can do it naturally in a fourth/fifth-dimensional setting, not third dimension, of course. We'd say that's impossible. So even if it's removed and it's removed from the third dimension, it still has the blueprint, and the energetic blueprint is a fourth/fifth-dimensional energy, and it's still there in the body. It can't be removed.

Q: What about a paralyzed arm? Can it function again fully?

C: Healing is possible. Healing of the physical body is possible no matter what level it's on, but in the third-dimensional setting, it can't take place. It can on the fourth/fifth dimension.

Q: One trend that we've seen is a growing number of people who are born autistic and some who do not speak at all. Perhaps the telepathic enhancements will allow us to interact with these groups?

C: That's absolutely correct. The fact is, those autistic kids who are coming in are carrying a very unique frequency of the New Dawning energy, and they are anchoring this energy onto the planet. That's part of their roles. They only work through telepathy. They've come here really to teach many of you how to open up and transmit that telepathic energy output. They embody that, and their presence on the planet at this time allows all of you to move into our telepathic abilities and to utilize them.

Q: You had talked about children being born with the crystalline structure. Could you talk about special needs children?

C: I feel very strongly that they are here to carry a unique frequency to help with the anchoring at this time. They have come in, not in fourth dimension, but they are in the other dimensional spaces anchoring in and transmitting energy out to human beings on the planet. So they are playing a very important role and they have come here to do that.

Q: I have a daughter with Down syndrome and this last year she has been so bad. Is she doing a lot of work somewhere else? Should I just be mellow?

C: I think what you need to understand is that she is spending more time "out" than "in." It is very hard for her to orientate herself because she is being almost aligned on the other dimensional sides, so there is a re-entry problem for her. I would look at finding someone who is working with energies to help her integrate when she comes back, so the re-entry into the third dimension is not so intense for her. She is really not of this world in lots of ways.

Q: I knew it. I always think she is an angel!

C: She is an angel and she has a beautiful heart. She came into this life to transmit that love out as a mirror for others, and she is doing a lot of important work here on the planet. You understand her and really claim her as she is.

Chapter 4

Q: Is telepathic communication used with words? How is the telepathic communion different?

C: The telepathic communion is more opening up to the God essence and aligning fully into the God essence of each person, which really is a higher frequency of telepathic use. That is what you are going to be activating and it allows you to become and move into a union of Oneness. Through the Oneness you experience that communion and telepathic communion. It has a very high multi-dimensional frequency of love. This is one aspect. The other one is telepathic communication, where you place your communication to another and receive an interaction of information between you. I've stated before that you need to start working with the natural forces first, or the Spiritual realms or the Pleiadians. You can sit in the Stargate form (which is in Chapter 10 of my first book). Your three Pleiadians will sit with you and between you. They take your hands energetically and you form the base of a pyramid energy, and go up into the Stargate chamber. In the Stargate chamber you actually can use your telepathic communion or telepathic communication with them. And with the telepathic center open you are going to be able to receive that translation from them very simply and easily because it's been re-opened now.

Chapter 5

Q: I live in an apartment and don't have a garden. Can I build my medicine circle inside?

C: Actually, no. The medicine circle needs to be outside on the earth. However, you can be creative with making your circles when you only have access to a public park, for example. You can find your place where there is not necessarily a lot of activity or a lot of people walking by, if that's possible. Anywhere you feel comfortable sitting on a blanket is good enough. Then create your circle; this can happen quickly when you've had the practice. Make your circle about the size of your blanket you'll be sitting on. You can use smaller stones in setting up your four directions. Once your circle is set up, bring in your blanket (your center stone will be the center of your blanket) and proceed. There you are, sitting in the park on your blanket having your experience. It's okay to play with this and let yourself open to the natural forces without having to have it be "perfect" before you work with a circle.

Q: How much corn meal do I use to seal my circle? Should I see this on the ground? Do I need to see the boundaries of my circle?

C: Good question. No, you don't have to "see" the boundaries of your circle. I know that will be hard for some of your ego minds. This will bring up a lot for some of you to be working in a space that doesn't have clear definitions. This is part of opening up to what you are creating with your circle, and that is fourth/fifth-dimensional spaces that are not a part of the third-dimensional limitations of the earth plane you have known up to this point.

So you want to sprinkle a little amount of corn meal along the edge of your circle as you create your seal. It is the smallest amount because you are just creating a fourth/fifth-dimensional seal to your circle.

Q: And how much tobacco do we put under a stone or place in each direction?

C: Again, very little. Only a pinch is required to give thanks or to send a prayer to Spirit. Don't let your ego mind interfere and come in with "the more I give the greater my thanks" or something along those lines. More is not better!

Q: If I can't find enough rocks to build my circle, can I use wood or branches of a tree?

C: Yes, of course. Rocks are always preferable. However, using branches or pieces of wood is okay. They will serve well in filling in your circle.

Q: I'm not clear about the doorway in the East. Which of the larger stones is the East? Or is the East direction the small stone that we move every time we go in and go out?

C: Your East direction is the smaller stone, yes. You are placing this smaller stone in the center of the two larger stones to create your doorway. That is your East direction. With that in mind, you really want to make sure you have larger stones on either side to anchor this direction. It's important to consciously choose the stones for your circle and be conscious of where they need to be placed in your circle. This may be your first communication with the natural forces, choosing your stones. Ask them if they want to be a part of your circle and where they want to be placed in the circle. You'll be surprised as they answer you! Make sure you give yourself enough space to be able to come in and out of your circle without disturbing these stones holding their position to anchor this direction.

Chapter 6

Q: What if I don't know my mission? It's not clear to me; I don't remember.

C: Everyone here has a role to play during these earth changes. And our first role is to birth our Self and then hold an anchor for many other human beings to follow in our footsteps during these changes. You have said yes to being here at this time. You have said yes to holding a certain space for this transformation to take place here. Sometimes you have to be reminded that you actually said yes to being here because during this transition time it can seem difficult. So you need to understand that you don't have anything to be afraid of, that all is in hand and you will play your role and things will unfold for each one of you here. You may not know all the details of your mission yet, but it is a privilege to be here on this earth plane at this time to hold an energetic space. You are birthing your Self into a new alignment, and as you do, energy goes out onto the earth plane to support and balance our energies here. It's really about consciously saying "Yes, I am birthing an aspect of myself here now. I am consciously doing this, and my human doesn't remember yet. I still have to work with my human aspect because I am having this human experience, and I have said yes to it."

Q: What does it mean when you say each one of us has said yes to being here at this time to fulfill our mission?

C: It means that you have to remember you are here to fulfill a mission that you said yes to. You have agreed to move into this expanded energy with the Galactic Council to accelerate our awakening. You carry a higher level of your own conscious light in the cells of your body and you act as transmitters for the planet and for people. You evolve to another level of consciousness of yourselves, not anyone else; it is just you birthing you.

Q: Do the Pleiadians give you a time frame for all of this?

C: I don't know the exact timing because Spirit is usually awful on time... because there is no such thing as time. You almost have to create a blueprint or a hologram, a template. By you activating yours, a template anchors on the earth plane. Every time you choose to be in the moment, that moment gets anchored onto the earth plane and allows another person to do it more easily. So you create these series of templates as you birth and evolve, and then as the others come up they will have a very different experience compared to you. You are the "way-showers"; you forge the path. Each one of you is forging the pathways for hundreds of human beings on this earth plane to follow, and that is what you each said yes to.

I wouldn't want to be anywhere else but where I am going, and doing what I am doing. This is my mission. You all have a mission here, each one of you.

Chapter 7

Q: Is it true that every human being on planet Earth comes from some-where else?

C: Home is not about an origin as far as meaning "where your original origin is." Home is about the Collective Consciousness and coming home to your place there. Every life force energy is a part of that Oneness.

Q: What happens when I do come back to my place of "home"? Do I leave the planet?

C: No, part of the New Dawning time is for you to have the experience, for you to return back to your alignment place to home, and at the same time live out your human experience here on the earth plane.

Q: Are there life force groups that we do not want to connect to, or do we have to connect to all of them?

C: All life force groups at this time are part of the divine Oneness, part of the Collective Consciousness. There are no life force groups in the Universe that are not a part of the Collective Consciousness, and because of this you can allow yourself to connect with all life force groups. The only negative energies in operation within the Universe right now are operating through planet Earth, and I am referring to those who are trying to control through misuse of power and violence.

Chapter 8

Q: I was completely lost in the crop circles process.

C: Completely lost is good; there is no attachment. Just Being, no interference. Sometimes you are moved in that direction. There comes a moment in the process where you understand. The crop circles have aligned to all the megalith sites and the megalith sites have every repositioning point aligned with the crop circles. Everything is lined up between them. The crop circles have redefined the sacred sites to their purest original form, and you, too, can be realigned to your pure and original form through the crop circles. The element that the Pleiadians want from you is for you to join this sacred webbing and add your essence to it because we need the human element. You are being asked to join that webbing and join that sacred connection.

Q: Will the megalithic sites upgrade and connection have any effect on the Earth changes that we are struggling with at this point?

C: Yes, it is going to transform things, but not before it shakes some things up initially. The Pleiadians are saying there are more Earth changes coming. The changes are going to accelerate because they need to at this time. There needs to be a redesign of our Earth energetically. Energetic lines are going to create shifts on the Earth where they need to take place. There's a lot of blockage in the Earth right now, pockets of energy within the Earth that are holding a dense congestion that really needs to be aligned to the dimensional space and the Earth itself. The soil of the Earth needs a true regeneration, because there is congestion of chemicals and pollution. Part of the regeneration process is not only to regenerate ourselves and our bodies, but to regenerate the life force of the Earth's soil. Everything needs to move and shift.

There will be a time of seeming chaos, and the last thing the Pleiadians want is to promote any fear, because there's been a lot of fear put out there about the Earth changes. The fact is, you don't have to be afraid. You just need to be mindful of being where you're supposed to be.

You hear people saying, "Oh, yeah, there's going to be mass exodus on the planet." There will be some people leaving the planet, but these are the people who aren't ready for peace. They aren't ready to move out of drama. They're into violence and power and control, and not in a small way. These people will be leaving the planet because they don't belong here anymore. They will take a step off the planet and have another experience, but they won't be staying here. That's just the way it is; that's how it was supposed to be.

Chapter 9

Q: How can we anchor grids on the earth?

C: The earth has a crystalline nature that is not the same as what we are carrying in our cells. It is a different one, but they can meet electrically and transfer and interact. You have the ability, as you activate the crystalline structure in you, to interact on a whole new level with the natural forces and the earth's energy, and to work on and within those grid lines. So anyone who is doing work with the earth as part of their mission is going to align energetically with those electrical grids and to move into their mission in a much more complete way.

Q: In this process of Crystalline Spinal Activation, can you talk more about the tapping?

C: The tapping is one of the pieces you will be working with to open the crystalline structure through the spine. You will work with that movement and the sound. The tapping is what is going to bring you in. The tapping will take you into the crystalline structure and it will open the doorway so your consciousness will go in.

Q: My mind wants to ask this: How can the position be here and the spine is in the back?
C: This is very third dimensional and it happens with the mind. You feel the pressure with your fingers on the position and the tapping opens the doorway for your Conscious Awareness to go in and through the back and into the spine to the crystalline structure. You might need to think of it that way for your ego mind so you are not sitting there wondering, *How am I going to do that?* So let's remedy this.

The tapping takes you to the dimensional space where the crystalline structure exists within the spine and the spine is very multidimensional. It takes you into the energy of the spinal fluid where the crystalline structure has been birthed. The spinal fluid is a sacred energy; it's a sacred fluid that is a birthing agent. Understand it is a very pure agent, pure essence. It has a very different frequency, a much higher frequency than any other crystalline structure in the body.

So as you tap, it takes you into a multi-dimensional element, which the spinal fluid holds. It is actually moving you into the spinal fluid to the crystalline structure. This opens the doorway into the crystalline structure. This is a truth.

So you tap, 1, 2, 3, and then bring your consciousness into the doorway created by that. Then you tap again, which will open you into another doorway. You are going to go through a series of gateways or doorways that take you into the dimensional setting where the crystalline structure exists within the spinal fluid.

You start here with a slight pressure, just below the soft opening at the base of the throat. It's at the very top of the sternum bone. Feel the soft opening and then move your fingers down to connect to the bone. Go past the indentation to where you have the solid sternum. Positioning is important. You start with a slight pressure and tap, 1, 2, 3, and that's it. With pressure on the sternum, you tap 1 and then you end up back on the sternum, and then you tap 2 and end up back on the sternum, and then you tap 3. This is going to create a quickening through you, so if you are feeling anxiety you may already feel the energy beginning to move through you. Take a breath into it.

Q: What is the purpose of our Command energy?
C: The Command Energy allows you to birth the activation of a healing movement within you, opens you into your natural healing energy, and allows you to access an experience of Oneness-Universal connection. As your cells begin to carry the essence of your Command Energy, the lungs expand with this

frequency of your Life Force Breath on another level, and your heart dimensionally expands. The crystalline structure within you transmits your Command Energy outward, making it possible for you to align into this transmitting energy force of your Self.

Q: Can you say more about the Command Energy?

C: You are going to be accessing what the Pleiadians call your Command Energy, so that you can consciously participate in your own birthing process and your own healing process. Now is the time that you consciously choose to activate another level of your crystalline structure within you and begin to utilize your Command Energy in your life. It's about calling your Command Energy forward, accessing a part of your Self to assist you in your own healing and mission.

You will be working within your heart center and using sacred sounds to activate a deep expansion and connection within the crystalline structure within your heart. As you work with this conscious alignment your crystalline factor within your heart will expand to a new level, to carry this essence of your Command Energy.

Through the portal you re-align back to an aspect of your personal power, to an aspect of your Command Energy. The new life force energy that you are receiving through the activation of your Command Energy is actually your own life force light, not anyone else's. It's yours coming from your own divine source into the cells of this body. It comes in increments that you can integrate and creates a gradual realignment back to Self. You will be opening up a conscious alignment with your Command Energy and anchor a stable access point within your heart for you to work from and anchor to. You always need to have a reason to activate your Command Energy, and to channel that desire with/beside your Command Energy.

Q: Why is it so important to integrate with nature while working with my Command Energy? How do I do this?

C: Understand the energies on the planet are creating a transformation with the natural forces and the activation of your crystalline structure will allow you to consciously harness this energy for the integration of your Command Energy through your cells.

The earth holds dimensional energies that can support your rapid expansion and assist you with integration within yourself. You can open up to the natural forces of the earth simply by bringing your conscious intention toward the earth while sitting or lying on the earth.

With each Conscious Breath that you take, feel the earth beneath you. Then let go with your breath. There will be an energetic breath that begins to create a synergy between you and the earth. Keep letting go into that connection so there is a weaving of energy between you and the earth. During this process a deep level of communion with the earth becomes possible, almost like telepathy. A loving link forms. When you open this link with the earth, the cells in your body can move through a deep healing and regeneration process.

Lie on the earth and allow your body to rest with these energies. Let go into the earth and allow yourself to be held by the earth while the wind and the sun work within your cells. Open to feel the heat of the sun on your body and bring a conscious communication toward the sun. You are birthing back into a remembrance of your spiritual nature. It is the time to use what is given to you, and as you do this more will be made available to you. This is the truth. We love and support you in your chosen journey.

Q: What if I am working in my Circle of Light and my dog comes in? Is that okay?

C: Of course. Understand the animal life force groups are connected to the fourth/fifth dimension, so your dog coming through will not disturb the energetics.

Q: I'm having trouble making my circle as I try to make bigger. Why does it looks more oval?

C: Stop and take a breath. That is the most common shape I have seen working with people. There have been many egg-shaped circles out there. The key is the make the distance between your crystals equal. That is the easiest way to ensure your shape is more circular and less oval.

Chapter 11

Q: Can you speak about the 12/12/12 and 12/21/12 energy or meaning?

C: 12/12/12 was another turning point on the earth plane. There were Illumination Waves that came onto the planet at that time. Now this was different from 11/11/11 where everyone received the crystalline structure and in that moment the third dimension shifted "off" for a short time. It's never going to come right back into its hold, so no one can quite get into the drama like they used to before that time. You try, but you can't quite be as dramatic as you used to be because of that shift.

On 12/12/12, the Illumination Waves were not for the masses. They were for a group of people specifically who were on the path to receive a level of Illumination and transformation through Conscious Choice, so 12/12/12 involved Conscious Choice. It was about consciously choosing to step forward and receive because this is the era.

On 12/12/12, those Illumination Waves were very specifically for the awakened group on the planet and 12/21/12 was another level of Illumination Waves. What you are receiving in this book will support you in creating a space for yourself through your energetic field by creating a series of energetic alignments. It's going to enable you to fully utilize the awakening energies of the Illumination Waves on a profound level. It's going to support you being able to stand and take a new place with yourself. And it is going to allow you to bring in a level of self-healing energy that will transform your cells to another level of awakening and energetic re-alignment to aspects of Self.

Q: When I was working with energetic alignment forms, two of the three were forms that I had worked with before. Is that okay? With the third one I thought, *Now I couldn't have made this one up!*

C: That's your ego mind again; it just wants to play a part. You know that; it always has a comment. Bring your Conscious Awareness into it and take a breath. It becomes even more defined. Enjoy the essence of what you are creating and get more involved. Trust it.

Q: My energetic alignment changes. Is that okay? And when do I use EE SHAH?

C: It is going to change; that is its stability. It will stay where it is, but it will change its form, and that will be completely normal. You use EE SHAH when it is fixed in its position, not in its form. When you feel like it is anchored, it still may be changing its form but it's not moving around—it's there. Bring all of your Self.

Q: If I feel it, can I bring my hands out more than three times?

C: You can, and you must go with your intuition. This is a structure, and there are pieces that are absolute, like having to do one infinity movement. If you do two it makes no difference. More is not better. It doesn't do anything; it is one that is required to be done properly. But if you have a sense that you need to make this movement again, honor that. It is your intuition. That's okay. You need to be creative and honor what is right for you in the moment.

Q: What if I'm not receiving anything from your sacred trust?

C: Realize there is always something waiting for you there, when you choose. Consciously choose to enter and to receive. If you are not feeling or sensing what is there for you, then you might not have fully integrated what you have received previously, so you are not ready to take another piece. Remember: You have to fully unwrap what you receive, and you do that by consciously bringing your attention to whatever is there for you and allow yourself to fully integrate this through you. There may be levels that you need to take in before you would want to access another piece.

Another possibility is that you didn't see what was there for you because you are in your head. So you can go back to that moment, the exact moment when you reached into your sacred trust and "nothing" was there, and from your heart space open to receive what is waiting there for you. There is no time, so that energy is still there waiting for you to receive. Take the time to really be in your heart before you go back to that moment and open up. Use the Conscious Breath and let go.

Chapter 12

Q: Within groups, does each person have his or her own mission?

C: Yes, and your biggest mission, which is often missed, is the unfolding of yourselves. To let go and allow the natural unfolding of your divine aspect and to love your human aspect and all that you are, all that you have been in this lifetime. This is everything. The moment you accept yourself with love, every part of your humanness, good and bad, a tremendous transformation takes place. Your enlightenment process happens very fast.

You are a series of experiences. That is what you have had since you were born. You need to love every part of the experiences that you have played. All your reactions, all the ways you have handled things, everything you have done—you need to embrace that and know you are human. Love that human experience and all that you are, whether you should have done it this way or that way. It's irrelevant. It was an experience; it was a choice you made. It is about honoring the experience and loving that vulnerable part of your Selves, the part of you that doesn't operate so well. The part that makes mistakes, that is afraid, that is sometimes angry or hurtful to others. It is the vulnerable, human part that needs your love, and that is where you need acceptance. Accept the imperfection. Hold your Selves with that love and compassion for the suffering that you have been a part of. The separation creates such suffering.

Be with what is in front of you in the moment. That is your next gift to unwrap. You can't push the gift away and say, "I don't want that one. I want this one." This is in front of you now, and it has been divinely orchestrated as your next step of learning. So you need to explore what is in front of you, to feel it, to breathe it, to touch it. Don't be afraid, because in truth there is nothing to be afraid of; there is just an experience to be felt. And the moment you have felt it and touched it and breathed it—it leaves and something else moves in.

This is your path, and at the same time you are moving into this awakening process. They go hand in hand. So many people want to push the humanness aside and be divine. You can't be divine if you are separated from your Self and you can't get away from you. You can go across to the other side of the world and guess what? You follow and you re-create everything around you the same because it's you.

Q: Are the "spiritual beings" the ones that tie everything together?

C: No, they are an aspect of the union of the Oneness. You have the Angels, Light Beings, and Masters, and you have the different energetic levels of the guides. They are working in alignment with their role of the Grand Plan, which fits into everybody else's role.

You have the Pleiadians and all the other alien energies that are coming in to play with their roles through different energies. Some of them are anchoring grids and doing work on the energetic field of the earth. Others are working through individuals or within groups of human beings. Then you have all the megalith sites on the planet, Stonehenge, the pyramids, all the sacred sites holding the ancient teachings and knowledge that are activating now, and the crop circles.

They are all part of the Grand Plan, and they are one of the life force groups of consciousness that are interacting with all. They are part of the Oneness, the God essence as well. So there is tremendous force and a clear plan of moving and working and re-creating the whole dimensional structure here.

One is not more important than the other; they don't work that way. Everyone is playing their role and it is designed for all of us to return back to our places within the Collective Consciousness so that we make up a conscious connection to our place in that Universal Grid.

Questions About the Processes

Q: What do I do if I'm not having an experience? I'm anxious because I'm not doing it right.

C: You're in your head. Your mind has comments, which means you're not in your body and you can't have the experience because your ego mind can't enter the fourth/fifth-dimensional energies. So it actually doesn't stop the energetic experience hitting your body, but it stops you from experiencing much.

Or it may be that you're in a rush. It's like you're trying to move things really, really fast instead of breathing slow and taking your time and giving yourself time, and your mind is kicking in also.

Or it may be that you have an agenda. And in the agenda, if you have one, you limit yourself automatically (when you have an agenda), because here you have an unlimited ability to have an experience on so many levels. The fact is, when you have an agenda in your mind of what you need to do or where you need to go, you instantly limit yourself and you limit your experience.

For example, yesterday you had an experience, so your mind is saying, "Well, let's go back to that. I like that experience." So you go through a similar process and you say, "Okay. I'm really looking forward to having this experience," and your entire mind focuses on that instead of being in the moment, in the experience that is presenting itself.

And my comment would be to you, why do you want the same experience as yesterday when you're ready for a completely different and new experience?
C: It's about really opening up and allowing yourself to fully receive yourself in the moment for what is being offered to you on this multi-dimensional level. You have so many multi-dimensional facets of your own light to experience; why would you want to experience the same thing? Why not take a breath and say, "Okay," and the words, "thy will be done." That says, "I surrender to the journey here and allow myself to be taken on this grand adventure."

Q: I have a fear that I will get so lost and I won't be able to catch up to your words if I just let go into my experience. Do I try and stay here?
C: Be aware for many of you this is a first-time process and it is good to be slow. Allow yourself to fully explore the space. Give yourself permission for that, because if you are slow in the beginning, guess what will happen? You will get very connected to the space and learn a lot about the essence of the space, and therefore you will soon get faster and faster. Don't break that down for yourself. It's only at the beginning that you really need to understand, and then you've got it all.

Q: I'm normally a visual person; I tend to see things. Now I feel like I am walking in the dark because I'm not receiving my usual visual. What do I do?
C: It's a good thing, actually. What they are saying is that you need to expand into your sensory energy, because there is a lot more for you in the sensory process than in the visual. Because you are moving into a whole new way of being, a whole new level of yourself on a dimensional level, sensory is the way to go. So they are asking for you to just be patient and to take a moment and close your eyes. Bring your Conscious Awareness and feel your way with your consciousness. Don't be impatient; just take the extra time and see what comes.

Q: What I sensed was thickness and warmth. And then in my mind I visualized a column.
C: You don't need to visualize. If it comes, fine, but don't try to make it happen because this limits it. You limit what you have the moment you decide

to make it a column. You disconnect from what actually is and then you don't receive it all. Once you see it as a column it's not the real thing and you are locked in no-man's land. So stay with the form even through it's a little frustrating. Touch it with your Conscious Awareness and just breathe into it to see, sense, or feel what it does. Build it with your breath and your consciousness rather than seeing. It will build a lot more elements within you. It feels really important.

Q: When I do a process, sometimes I feel myself going "out" and I lose your words. Do I bring myself back or let myself go with my experience?

C: It is your experience that gives you your answers. Your direct experience is everything. Words actually mean very little. What I want you to do in each process is not to necessarily listen to my words, but to go with your experience. If you lose my voice it is because you are where you are supposed to be. Don't try to get back to my voice; go in the direction you are being taken for your initiation.

If something doesn't feel okay to you, then it is not. The fact is, you might feel uncomfortable with something and it is important for you to honor yourself and not always comply with what I am saying. This is about you and your power, you and your intuition, and honoring that. So I want to say that to you because it's very important to me that *you are here for you*; you are not following like a herd of sheep. This is an individual process and you are unique. You will have your own unique way. It may vary a little from what I am saying. It is essential that you just say "Okay, this is my experience and I am honoring me in the experience."

If something really doesn't feel okay and I am saying, "Do X," you can decide it doesn't feel good for you to do that, and you work out what does feel good for you. You get to do your own unique process within the process.

Q: The last few times I did the processes, I fell asleep.

C: Good. That's perfect. And it wasn't sleep; it was a sleep-like state, which takes you into a very pure initiation that cannot be interfered with. That is a very good thing. And it may happen again. You are on a fast track.

Q: The last time I did the process I felt as though my mouth was watering, like I was drooling.

C: Feels like an energetic manna coming in to support the crystalline activation through you.

Q: What can I do when my mind comes in and tries to relate to what is coming?

C: Don't try to make it into something because that shuts things down. You go back to third dimension so you can't work because you are in that third-dimensional setting. Be very patient and loving toward your mind and say, "You are not doing this right now" and come down to your heart. Bring your energy there; when you feel yourself there, continue. Your experience will wait for you.

Q: Can you talk more about the sacred sound and the thought code?

C: You are going to be working with these two components. The sacred sound is something that you are actually going to be speaking; you are going to bring the sound forth into the crystalline structure. You can bring the sound forward in many forms; you cannot change the configuration of the sound, but you can change the emphasis of how you bring forth the sound, so that at some point you become the sound and the sound becomes you.

Then there is a sacred code, which is like a thought code that you actually place in the crystalline structure with your consciousness. It holds a higher frequency of vibration than the actual sound. It is a telepathic thought code that you will place, not speak.

General Questions

Q: Is everyone going to go through this transformation? Even the people who are focused on survival and who don't necessarily have access to any of this information?

C: Everyone, regardless of living in a shack or a mansion, will go through the transformation in his or her own way. Every human being had that crystalline structure anchored through them on 11/11/11 regardless of what money they had or who they were. Everyone has that in readiness for the dimensional shift on the earth plane when it comes in its fullness. So you really don't want to be distracted by everyone out there and their experience, because they are playing their role. Where you need to be is with yourselves and with our own unfolding. Everything is in hand for every human being on this earth plane to move into their transformation.

Q: Do you feel like the healing modalities need to change or are we to do our own healing?

C: What I find is if you're connected to your heart, and whatever healing modality you're using, you're going to find an intuitive expansion on everything that you're doing right now, because the changing times are bringing opportunities for you to transform your healing modalities.

And if you're connected, then you're going to get insight and understanding into new ways of doing things, expanded ways of doing things, and you will bring changes within that healing modality that will bring in and channel through a lot of the new energies that are here for the earth. That's what I see you need to do.

All you need to surrender to is your heart; just open up to the energy and just allow yourself your creativity. It's the creativity of your divine light that can come in and transform the healing modalities that are in place right now. So if you are open to that, just call on the spiritual realms to support you in that and show you the next step. You have to open to it. You have to reach out now. It is time to do that. And you can. You will be received, and you will get the information you need.

Q: You spoke of energies of the Pleiadians supporting us through this shift. Are there any energies that are not supporting us through this shift?

C: No, I don't see that anymore. It's like the karma has gone, and now you are supported in this whole shift in consciousness. And the whole Universe is looking toward you now and supporting you at this time. And, of course, to the Pleiadians, it's a very fast transition. Because you on earth are so caught up in time, it's different, but it's a very quick thing for them, and they're watching it with great interest and support.

Q: Can you share how the Pleiadians are working with us?

C: You are generally allocated a team of three Pleiadians that come together for each person. So when people get together in a project there is an expanded dynamic that's perfectly done. The Pleiadians are very much into sacred geometry; everything is set out in a sacred geometric form. That is how the vortexes are built and that is how they work.

So if you have a group of three humans and three Pleiadians, you have nine Pleiadian energies that will set out a geometrical form and anchor your project through the channel of that form. That is like a magnifier that brings a channeled force through that is part of the synergy of your group.

Q: How can we connect more with the Pleiadians and actually meet them?

C: In Chapter 3 on Formations in my first book, you can sit with the Pleiadians and work with the Pleiadians. They actually come and sit with you in the formation and they activate a sacred geometrical form that you can work with, and it's all laid out in the book. In Chapter 10 you go into the Stargate energies, which is an expanded formation in which you connect with the Pleiadians on a deeper level.

Q: What do they mean when they talk about the master numbers?

C: They hold a frequency, certain numbers and geometrical forms, but language is not that simple. Your language is limited so it's much more—I wouldn't say complex because it's a pure essence truth that is in a frequency form that is not complicated at all—it's just different for our language to be able to have a concept of it. It is beyond the third/fourth/fifth/sixth dimension. It's more into the ninth/tenth-dimensional element and not something you have a concept of yet.

Q: Why are there so many crop circles in England?
C: You see it as "in England" and the Pleiadians see it as an energetic space on the earth plane that is holding a certain geometrical form and pattern rather than it being a country. They see it very differently.

Q: How do I answer my child when asked what is going to happen on the planet? Right now I am saying, "Everything is going to be okay," and I'm wondering if that is enough.
C: Well, on some level they already know that something is coming and all you are doing with that answer is adding to the anxiety, and then they can no longer trust you. They have no point of reference that they can trust. So it is important to not tell them "Everything is going to be okay"—it actually *is* going to be okay, but there is a lot of fear that has been put out there and not all of it is accurate. It's important to explain the full picture of the story rather than the drama of what is put out there, creating a tremendous amount of fear. It's best to share that they have a good heart and all those with good hearts will be okay and will be safe here on the earth plane. You will all be taken care of. You're here at a special time of transformation. Move the focus away from the drama and destruction to the truth of the times and the transformation of the times.

Lying to a child does not help. Give them information based on truth and then their heart can receive and know, and then feel calmed by it. With understanding and clarity fear disappears.

Q: Do we disappear in the Oneness?
C: In that ocean of light, you are a drop of the ocean, and as you go into that ocean of light as a drop, you become so much more defined in who you are. You never get lost in the ocean. You just become more and more within your Selves. And that's one of the reasons that until now you're held back from union with each other—this concept that you will be lost. That is just not a truth.

You will start to realize that you become even more defined, that you're unique in the universe, and you hold a unique, important place. You will start to experience this in a group, and you will experience that it allows you to take bigger steps for your Self.

As your frequency pulses out from your heart it's going to keep pulsing out the Universal Consciousness. That Universal Collective Energy is going to recognize you through your unique frequency of light and, as it recognizes it, it's going to align your Self to an energetic flow of connection. The Universe will begin to align you to that natural flow where you need to be—your own river of light, so to speak, and a new pathway is forged for you to birth into almost like a flowing light river. You are on your own unique frequency being bathed by this light and taken into the ocean of light.

My experience with this was that I became more brilliant, more defined, within who I was. I had the most profound experience of myself. Don't hold back. Trust in your own unique place in it all.

Appendix B:
Ongoing Work With Christine

I want to share the numerous avenues available for you to receive this material so that you can experience the latest teachings and information that is coming from the Pleiadians. You can join me at *www.christinedayonline.com*.

Transmissions

Transmissions are energetic sessions channeled by the Pleiadians. The Transmissions begin with a channeled dialogue from the Pleiadians, so each Transmission tends to work with a theme, and each Transmission is completely different from the other.

These Transmissions create healing and energetic transformations, initiating you into a higher level of your light. They are highly transformational and allow you to take another step toward your Self. They work by transmitting healing light out to large groups of people, so everyone within the area receives these energies of light.

These transmissions of light open up initiations for you—initiations of the Self through your cells. This can create healing through the physical body and the emotional body, and create new levels of spiritual awakening for each individual.

Transmissions are held in different venues throughout the world and are open to the general public.

Three-Day Pleiadian Seminars

The Pleiadians have opened a series of initiations throughout a three-day period specifically designed for the general public. These initiations include activating your crystalline structure for telepathic communion with the Pleiadians, the Lemurians, and all Galactic energies. Through working with a powerful crystal vortex you are able to re-align to aspects of your sacred Self and begin a multi-dimensional experience as you journey within the dimensional light activated through the crystal vortex.

You will be working directly with the Pleiadians in the Stargate chamber. These events bring you in direct contact with the Pleiadians, forming a personal relationship with them during the three days.

You will be given step-by-step processes of learning tools with which you can navigate into a deeper communication with the Pleiadians, the Lemurians, and all Galactic energies, as well as the Spiritual realms.

We work in alignment with the crop circles and energetic portals with the Pleiadians within the crystalline vortex to receive a series of awakening codes for a rapid transformation of Self. The cells of your body go through a rejuvenation process as the awakening codes are received. The sacred Matrix is also a sacred aspect connected by the crop circles for your transformation. We will be working within the sacred Matrix journey for an advanced awakening.

All energies from the spiritual realms are able to come and assist in these events because of the series of dimensional energies that are anchored, creating an energetic womb within the room that you are held in as you birth. It allows the Angels, Light Beings, and Masters to come into the workspace and assist you in your transformations.

Know that there is a place held for each one of you who choose to come to this event for your next step. I look forward to all of you called to be part of this experience.

Pleiadian Shamanic Retreats

The Pleiadians say that in order to fully complete the self-realization process of our Oneness with all the life force energies that exist within the Universe, we must first remember and rebuild our sacred relationship with the natural forces. Indeed, the natural forces have an essential role to play in our integration of this new awakening consciousness that is transforming the cells of our body into light.

In this three-day Pleiadian Shamanic Retreat, you will be introduced to Sacred Ritual Initiations through the Pleiadian energies. We will be working with the Galactic Council through a series of energetic portals that have been specifically set up for you to open into a pure alignment and communication with all the star energies within the Galaxy.

In this time of New Dawning, there is an opportunity for you to birth into a new level of consciousness that will enable you to experience deeper communication with the earth and all the natural forces.

You will learn through Pleiadian tools how to harness the energies of the earth, wind, fire, water, and the sun that take you on a transformative journey and enable you to create an entirely new experience and relationship to these natural elemental forces. You will utilize the time-honored Medicine Wheel and Fire ceremonies, as well as energetic portals to create a transformative experience.

You will connect with the Pleiadians and the Galactic Council, who will be present throughout the event to assist you in reconnecting to your own powerful energetic force.

Tele-Seminars

At the request of the Pleiadians these tele-seminars will be 90 minutes in length, and they will be scheduled at regular intervals of two per month. They are designed to bring you on a sacred journey of initiation.

Each tele-seminar will bring to you:

- The latest information from the Pleiadians.
- Energetic theme and content.
- A set of tools for your work.
- A way to utilize these tools within an initiation Transmission. I will be channeling the powerful light energies for you to experience and birth.
- A time for questions.

There will be a set of six tele-seminars. Each set of six has been designed to contain an important theme for your resurrection process. Each individual tele-seminar builds on this theme, so that you can expand the tools and direct experience within the initiations in each class.

You may attend only one tele-seminar that will bring you into a powerful initiation experience. Each one is complete in itself, so that you can join in any one tele-seminar class that calls you. These tele-seminars begin January 2014. For more information about the dates of these events visit my Website at *www. christinedayonline.com.*

Christine Day on the Awakening Zone

Join Christine live on the first and third Monday of each month from 2:30 to 4 p.m. USA Central Time, for more enlightening information and energetic keys from the Pleiadians. As we move deeper into the transition that is taking place on planet Earth, the Pleiadians tell us that the time has come to start mastering the energetic tools that will enable us to consciously complete our awakening and self-healing process in preparation for 2013 and beyond. In this new twice-monthly show I present a new body of information and transmissions of sacred tones and codes specifically designed to act as energetic keys to unlock the information residing within the matrix of your cellular structure.

Shows are available to listen to or download from the Archives at the Awakening Zone Network. Look for Pleiadian Tools for Self Realization at *www. awakeningzone.com.*

Pleiadian Broadcasts

The Pleiadian Broadcasts are available at regular intervals throughout the year on my Website. To view the show go *www.christinedayonline.com.* The broadcasts are typically aired six times a year. This is a unique opportunity to work with the teachings and tools from the Pleiadians, which they bring forth specifically for this format. You are able watch the show from your home and view the material and processes as they are presented. The broadcasts are then made available for you to work with the tools and teachings as you feel called to and at your own pace. All the broadcasts are available for you to view or download for free.

Newsletter

Each month I send out a newsletter with a message from the Pleiadians and from me. I give a brief synopsis of what I am doing and what the Pleiadians are bringing for you to take your next steps. Visit my Website at *www.christineday-online.com* to sign up!

About the Work

Again, it feels important that I talk about, and describe to you, the two bodies of work that were channeled to me so long ago and that are currently being offered in many areas of the world today.

Amanae was the first channeled work that I anchored into the world. Amanae is a hands-on, multi-dimensional bodywork process that opens up the emotionally held blocks in the body. Amanae opens up a direct access for you to connect to your emotions that are held in your physical body. As you consciously feel this emotion, it can leave your body, and healing can take place. This moves the body into healing on many different levels, within the physical and emotional bodies. And there is a deep spiritual transformation that takes place as the emotion moves out, and the light of the Self anchors into your cells.

Frequencies of Brilliance was channeled through me, and birthed at the exact same moment as Amanae. At the time these two bodies of work were anchored through me, I was told humans were not ready for this second body of work, so it was not to be transmitted on to the earth plane at that time. Thirteen years later, in 1999, I was told to begin teaching and initiating people in this work. I have been initiating practitioners and teachers in this work ever since, and it has been my main work on the earth plane up to this time.

In this new dawning time I am being asked to begin a new path, working closely with the Galactic energies which include the Pleiadians, and many other Star energies. I am currently undergoing a powerful initiation of communication through multi-dimensional portals to enable me to open into new Galactic communications.

I am being asked to align to higher multi-dimensional states in order for me to begin to open into higher states of Truth to be able to bring through information and sacred knowledge that we as human beings are ready to receive now.

I have been put on notice that I will begin my initiation process with the publication of this book and it will take some months to be ready energetically to be able to carry this powerful inter galactic communication within me.

I am committed to my next step of my mission.

I look forward to passing on this information, to all that are ready to receive, as it is made available to me.

So Be It!

Index

Activating your Command Energy, 124-125

Activating your crystalline structure, 35-47

Activation of your telepathic center, 50-54

Active blueprint, 25-26

Alien energies, 74

Aligning to your mission, 74-83

Alignment, 14, 54, 62, 96,145-156

Alignments, network of, 36

Alliance energies, 75

Alliances, energetic, 31, 33, 120, 130-144, 147

Anchoring home, 87, 88-90

Angels, 22, 31, 50, 76, 146

Animal kingdom, 21, 50

Atlantians, 38, 146

Atlantis, 38

Awakening codes, 108-109, 110

Awareness, 19

Birthing process, 20, 22, 35, 36, 9, 50, 77, 85, 87, 98

Blueprint, 25-26, 98-104, 131-132, 138-139

Brain, the, 39-40, 48

Buddha, 31

Circle of light, 125-129

Code Forms, 52, 53, 66-67

Collective Consciousness, 10, 14, 15, 24, 25-26, 30, 31, 38, 41, 48, 55, 75, 84, 96, 99, 101, 131-132

Command Energy, 118-129, 130-144, 147

Communication, telepathic, 39-40, 48-59

Communion Conferences, 110-111

Communion with nature, 60-72

Communion, telepathic, 48-59, 76, 84-94, 134

Completion energy, 146

Conscious Awareness, 40, 51, 52, 66, 110, 137

Conscious Breath, 47, 51, 121

Conscious Choice, 19, 24-34, 35, 37, 38, 61, 84, 118-129, 130, 131, 135

Crop circles, 36, 76, 95-106, 107

Crystalline energy, 85

Crystalline structure, 15, 22, 48, 49, 50, 51, 52, 54, 100-101, 109, 11-112, 119, 120, 122, 123-124, 133
Crystalline structure, activating your, 35-47
Destiny line, 131-132, 138
Destiny, 74-83
Dimensional codes, 81
Direction, elements of each, 71-73
Divine Access Point, 43
Divine factor, 40
Divine intuition, 41
DNA, 130
Earth (element), 62, 65-66
Ego, 85, 86
Energetic alliances, 31, 33, 120, 130-144, 147
Energetic portals, 118-129
Energy, completion, 146
Fear, 19
Fifth dimension, 17, 18, 21, 27, 28, 33, 35-36, 37, 48, 51, 85, 95, 97, 134, 146, 156
Fire (element), 62, 65
Forces, natural, 62, 64-73, 133, 141-142
Fourth dimension, 17, 18, 21, 25, 28, 33, 35-36, 37, 48, 51, 85, 95, 97, 134, 146
Frequency, light, 97
Frequency, sound, 98
Galactic Council, 31, 74, 76, 78
Gifts, natural, 48
God Consciousness, 54, 74
Godhead consciousness, 112
Grand Plan, 74, 76, 77, 98
Great Pyramids, 96, 97
Group consciousness, 54-55
Hand muhdrah, 52

Healers, 75
Heart center, 130-144
Heart, the, 41-42, 45-47, 51, 84-85, 86-87, 123
Holographic designs, 107-108
Home, 86-87, 88-90, 121, 146
Human aspect, 17-23
Hypothalamus, 40, 48
Internal separation, 19-20, 21
Jesus, 20, 22, 31, 49
Kundeline energy, 42
Lack, 85
Lemurians, 31, 38, 49, 50, 54, 101, 112, 146
Life Force Breath, 121, 132-133
Life force groups, 21-22
Life force groups, 50, 74, 84-94
Light Beings, 22, 31, 50, 76, 146
Light frequency, 97
Light signatures, 136-137
Light Workers, 75
Light, 16
Light, circle of, 125-129
Masters, 31, 50, 76, 146
Matrix, the sacred, 107-117
Medicine circle, 67-71
Megalith sites, 36, 76, 96-97
Memory of home, 88-90
Memory, 42
Mineral kingdom, 21, 50
Mission, aligning to your, 74-83
Mistakes, 19
Mother Earth, 61, 63, 65-66, 70
Mother Mary, 20, 22, 31, 49, 100, 148
Natural forces, 50, 62, 64-73, 133, 141-142
Natural gifts, 48
Nature, sacred communion with, 60-72

Nervous system, 42

Network of alignments, 36

New Dawing, 10, 13, 17, 18, 19, 24,
        35, 36, 39, 41-42, 50, 54, 61,
        62, 74, 75, 95-96, 107, 121,
        122, 135, 136, 146

Oneness, 21, 22, 28, 25, 38, 50, 52, 54,
        76, 83, 109, 121, 133-134,
        147, 156

Perfection, 19-20, 156

Pineal gland, 40, 48

Plant kingdom, 21, 50

Pleiadians, 9, 11, 18, 22, 27, 31, 35,
        38, 40, 41, 49, 50, 51, 54, 60,
        61, 62, 63, 76, 86, 95, 98, 101,
        107, 118, 132, 136, 145, 146, 149

Power, 24

Pre-agreements, 13, 14, 16, 17, 24-34,
        36, 38, 49, 54, 74, 110, 145-146,
        149, 151-152

Quan Yen, 31

Responsibility, 24

Resurrection process, 22

Sacred blueprint, activating, 101-104

Sacred geometry, 97

Sacred heart receiver, 118

Sacred heart, 21, 41

Sacred matrix, the, 107-117

Sacred sound, 15, 51, 120

Sacred trust, 131-133, 139-141

Sacred, being, 17-23

Sai Baba, 22, 31, 49

Self-acceptance, 18

Self-condemnation, 18, 148

Self-empowerment, 48

Self-Healing Prophecy, 35

Self-healing, 20

Self-judgment, 18

Self-resurrection, 147

Serians, 50, 146

Shamanic worlds, 136

Sixth dimension, 134

Sound frequency, 98

Spine, the, 42-43, 111-112

Star beings, 75

Star energies, 31, 146

Stargates, 97

Stonehenge, 96

Sun (element), 62, 64-65

Telepathic center, 39

Telepathic center, activation of your,
        50-43

Telepathic communication, 39-40,
        48-59

Telepathic communion, 48-59, 76,
        84-94, 134

Template Energy, 77-78, 85

Template, activating your, 78-81

Thalamus, 40, 48

Third dimension, 18, 21, 22, 25, 27,
        28, 50-51, 54, 84, 85, 97, 112,
        120, 121, 134, 145

Thought code, 52

Thought transference, 51

Thyroid, the, 40-41, 43-45

Universal Consciousness, 14-15, 16,
        25-26, 39, 40, 41, 48, 50, 77-78

Universal Grid, 82-83, 121, 146, 156

Warrior Self, 61-64, 67

Wind (element), 62, 65